Guideline for Sustainable Energy Efficient Architecture & Construction

Young Cities Research Paper Series, Volume 10

Klaus Rückert, Effatolsadat Shahriari

Young Cities Research Paper Series, Volume 10
Edited by Technische Universität Berlin and
Road, Housing & Urban Development Research Center, Tehran

German-Iranian Research Project
Young Cities
Developing Energy-Efficient Urban Fabric in the Tehran-Karaj Region

Contact Germany	**Contact Iran**
Young Cities Project Center	BHRC Road, Housing & Urban
Technische Universität Berlin	Development Research Center
Secr. A 66	P.O. Box 13145-1696
Straße des 17. Juni 152	Sheikh Fazlollah Noori Highway
10623 Berlin | Germany	Tehran | Islamic Republic of Iran
www.youngcities.org	www.bhrc.ac.ir

Design/Typesetting büro-d | Communication Design Berlin

Publisher

Universitätsverlag der TU Berlin	BHRC
Universitätsbibliothek	P.O. Box 13145-1696
Fasanenstr. 88	Sheikh Fazlollah Noori Highway
10623 Berlin | Germany	Tehran | Islamic Republic of Iran
www.univerlag.tu-berlin.de	www.bhrc.ac.ir
ISSN 2193-6099 (Print)	ISBN 978-600-113-114-1
ISSN 2193-6102 (Online)	
ISBN 978-3-7983-2677-4 (Print)	
ISBN 978-3-7983-2678-1 (Online)	

Also published online on the Digital Repository
of the Technische Universität Berlin
URL http://opus4.kobv.de/opus4-tuberlin/frontdoor/index/
 index/docId/4716
URN urn:nbn:de:kobv:83-opus4-47167
[http://nbn-resolving.de/urn:nbn:de:kobv:83-opus4-47167]

All texts based on scientific research by the Young Cities project.
All pictures, tables and graphics are courtesy of the respective article's
authors despite any other courtesy is indicated.

© 2014 All rights reserved by the Technische Universität Berlin.

Young Cities Research Paper Series

Editors: Rudolf Schäfer, Farshad Nasrollahi, Holger Ohlenburg, Cornelia Saalmann, Florian Stellmacher

List of Volumes

01 Accomplishments and Objectives (in Farsi)
Rudolf Schäfer, Tayebeh Parhizkar, Farshad Nasrollahi, Holger Ohlenburg, Ghazal Raheb, Florian Stellmacher (Eds.)

02 Accomplishments and Objectives (in English)
Rudolf Schäfer, Farshad Nasrollahi, Holger Ohlenburg, Florian Stellmacher (Eds.)

03 The Shahre Javan Community Detailed Plan
Elke Pahl-Weber, Sebastian Seelig, Holger Ohlenburg (Eds.)

04 Energy Efficient Housing for Iran
Farshad Nasrollahi, Philipp Wehage, Effatolsadat Shahriari, Abbas Tarkashvand

05 Urban Challenges and Urban Design
Elke Pahl-Weber, Sebastian Seelig, Holger Ohlenburg, Nadine Kuhla von Bergmann (Eds.)

06 Construction Competencies and Building Quality
Bernd Mahrin, Johannes Meyser (Eds.)

07 New Towns—Promises Towards Sustainable Urban Form
Mohammad Reza Shirazi

08 Green Office Buildings
Farshad Nasrollahi

09 Intelligent Design using Solar-Climatic Vision
Mojtaba Samimi, Farshad Nasrollahi

10 Guideline for Sustainable Energy Efficient Architecture & Construction
Klaus Rückert, Effatolsadat Shahriari

Bibliographic information published by the Deutsche Nationalbibliothek
The Deutsche Nationalbibliothek lists this publication in the Deutsche Nationalbibliografie; detailed bibliographic data are available in the Internet at http://dnb.dnb.de

Acknowledgments

This publication is prepared in the frame of Young Cities Research Paper Series, connected to the Young Cities project, one of the projects under the umbrella of "Megacities of Tomorrow".

The interdisciplinary research project "Young Cities–Developing Energy-Efficient Urban Fabric in the Tehran-Karaj Region" was funded by the German Federal Ministry of Education and Research (BMBF), as well as the Iranian Ministry of Roads & Urban Development (MRUD) (former Ministry of Housing and Urban Development). Therefore we would like to thank earnestly the German Federal Ministry of Education and Research to provide a valuable frame and space for us to develop our ideas about sustainability. We would like also to thank sincerely the Technische Universität Berlin and the Road, Housing & Urban Development Research Center of Iran (former Building and Housing Research Center, BHRC) to enable the project in a scientific atmosphere.

Our special thanks are for the project directors Dr. Tayebeh Parhizkar from BHRC Tehran and Prof. Rudolf Schäfer from the Technische Universität Berlin, who guided and supported the project genuinely.

Following several years of research and developing climate responsive, energy efficient residential pilot projects, to strengthen and support sustainable buildings particularly in Iran and generally in the MENA region, the guideline for sustainable and energy efficient architecture and construction is developed. This publication and the residential pilot projects have been performed at the department of design and structure (tek) chair of Prof. Dr.-Ing. Klaus Rückert. The developed guideline is a product of team work and friendly support of colleagues in tek. We are especially grateful to tek secretary Kerstin Eckstein and also Ing. Jan Grunwald and Ph.D. Candidate Kamran Naeiji for the scientific support.

We would like to express our gratitude to our student assistants Olga Gordashnik who prepared the graphics and drawings of residential pilot projects and Daniel Mera who have prepared the illustrations and drawings of this volume.

We would also like to sincerely thank Amir Vedadi, who supported this publication by precise proofreading. Our special thanks are for our colleagues in the Young Cities project center, Cornelia Saalmann and Mathias Orth-Heinz, who their strong supports made this publication possible. Our further gratitude is again for Cornelia Saalmann as a member on the Board of Editors of Young Cities Research Paper Series, who is the editor of this volume. We would also like to thank büro-d for the layout and graphics design of the guideline.

The German side of the Young Cities project is partly funded by German Federal Ministry of Education and Research (BMBF).

SPONSORED BY THE

Table of Contents

Forewords
R. Schaefer 12
T. Parhizkar 13

I Introduction **14**
1 **Guideline for Integrated Planning Team** **18**
2 **Definition and Motivation** **19**
2.1 Environmental Impact of Convenience Approach . . . 19
2.2 Benefits of Applying the Guideline 19

II Sustainable Design Strategies **22**
1 **Basic Terms and Definitions** **26**
1.1 Climate and Thermal Comfort 26
1.2 Relations between Outdoor and Indoor Comfort . . . 27
1.3 Relation between Climate and Building 27
2 **Principles** **30**
2.1 Orientation 30
2.2 Daylighting 34
2.3 Shading 36
2.4 Storing the Sun Energy-Sunspaces 37
2.5 Thermal Mass and Insulation 39
2.6 Natural Ventilation 40
2.7 Airtightness 40

III Sustainable Construction **44**
1 **Main Pillars of Sustainable Construction** **48**
2 **Construction Systems** **50**
2.1 Block Work, Brick Infill 50
2.2 Block Work, Lightweight Block Infill 52
2.3 Conventional Panels 53
2.4 Light Weight Steel Frame 54
2.5 Tunnel Form Structural System 55
2.6 Precast Modular 57

3	**Building Elements**	**59**
3.1	Foundations and Footings	59
3.2	Walls	60
3.3	Floors	61
3.4	Roofs	62
3.5	Doors	64
3.6	Windows	66
IV	**Ecological Building Materials**	**68**
1	**Criteria for Selecting Materials**	**71**
2	**Ecological Materials for Sustainable Construction**	**75**
3	**Most Common Constructional Materials**	**76**
3.1	Concrete	76
3.2	Timber	77
3.3	Aluminum (Frame)	78
3.4	PVC (Frame)	79
3.5	Wooden (Frame)	80
3.6	Metal	81
4	**Finishing Materials**	**82**
4.1	Clay Plaster	82
4.2	Lime Plaster	83
5	**Insulation**	**84**
5.1	Most Common Insulation Materials	85
5.2	Glass Wool	86
5.3	Rock Wool	87
5.4	Keramzite or Ceramic	88
5.5	Foam Polymer Materials	89
5.6	Cellulose	90
5.7	Wood Fiber	91
5.8	Flax and Hemp	92
5.9	Sheep Wool	93
5.10	Types of Insulation	94

V Applicable Measures for Building Physic 98
1 Insulation 101
1.1 General Principles 101
1.2 Design Consideration 102
2 Glass and Glazing 105
2.1 General Principles 105
2.2 Types of Glazing 107
2.3 Thermal Performance of Different Glazing Types 110
2.4 Design Consideration 112
3 Thermal Mass 115
3.1 General Principles 115
3.2 Combined Types of Thermal Mass 117
3.3 Typical Thermal Mass Applications 120
3.4 Design Consideration 122
4 Daylighting 124
4.1 General Principles 124
4.2 Design Consideration 125
5 Shading and Avoiding Overheating 129
5.1 General Principles 130
5.2 Types of Shading 134
5.3 Shading and Daylight 138
5.4 Design Consideration 140
6 Ventilation 144
6.1 General Principles 146
6.2 Types of Ventilation 151
6.3 Design Consideration 153
7 Airtightness 157
7.1 General Principles 157
7.2 Advantages of Airtight Building 159
7.3 Design Consideration 160

VI Appendix 164
List of References 166
List of Figures 173
List of Tables 176
List of Abbreviations 177
Young City Project Consortium 178
About the Authors 180

Forewords

Architects, designers and building developers concentrate more and more on the issues of sustainability in general and energy and resource efficiency, climatic response and cultural sensitivity in particular as the main indicators of building quality in recent years.

From this perspective, a guideline for sustainable energy efficient architecture and construction with especial attention to social and cultural backgrounds is an essential part of an environmental friendly approach.

Following this fundamental approach, this publication aims at introduction of an appropriate guideline with energy efficiency and cost efficiency as key issues (the later issue is demonstrated through adopting passive solar architecture and construction principles). Through this guideline the adopted principles, optimal strategies and architectural and constructional measures will be introduced to architects, building designers and developers in Iran and MENA region. Final outcomes of applying such a guideline would lead to less: ecological impact of building on environment, energy consumption, resource consumption, and life cycle cost.

This guideline in fact, reflects the results and findings of the research and design phase. It would be an appropriate tool for architects, engineers and building developers who care about environmental issues. Even though the focus of the guideline is on Iran and Tehran region; by considering specific climate conditions of each case, the introduced criteria, methods, measure and materials could be applicable to MENA region as well.

This publication consists of basic topics for designing, developing and building an energy efficient, environmental friendly and high quality building; namely: the necessity of sustainable approach, sustainable design strategies, pillars of sustainable construction including construction system, building elements, ecological building materials and applicable measures for building physic.

Prof. Dr. Rudolf Schaefer

The considerable growth of population in Tehran region and other mega cities has emphasized on the necessity of providing the housing in these cities. According to the statistics in the last few years, considering the young age average of Iran's population, around 1.5 million housing units are needed every year. These statistics, along with the concentration of the population in mega cities such as Tehran, requires basic solutions. Furthermore, the quality of construction in Iran is another important issue which has great impact on environment and could cause more problems in mega cities of Iran in general and Tehran in particular.

Tehran is one of the most important mega cities, for which the development of a new town has been centered around. New Towns provide valuable capabilities and facilities for designers and developers. Appropriate use of such opportunities can lead to forming proper patterns for the urban development as well as promoting appropriate construction methods and systems in construction industry of the country.

The same as other developing countries, it is necessary to concentrate more on the issues such as sustainability in general and energy and resource efficiency in particular as the key indicators of construction and building quality, and support this approach through governmental institutions.

Considering this approach, a guideline for sustainable energy efficient architecture and construction could be a suitable tool for those who are involved in construction industry from different aspects. Through this guideline, the key principles, optimal strategies and architectural and constructional measures will be discussed and introduced to building designers and developers in Iran and MENA region.

This volume of the Young Cities Research Paper series presents a broad overview on the strategies and measures which are outcomes and findings of the research and design phase of the project. It covers whole span of the building life cycle, as from preliminary concepts to developing construction strategies. It aims to promote higher quality of construction by covering issues such as: importance of sustainable approach, introduction of sustainable strategies, pillars of sustainable construction and finally ecological materials and measures for building physic.

Dr. Parhizkar

I
Introduction

Introduction

Designing, construction, implementation, operation and maintaining residential buildings without considering sustainable principles and measures, normally requires huge amounts of energy, natural resources and more importantly water. In addition to producing massive amounts of waste, whole procedure of construction drastically damages the environment. Furthermore, running phase of buildings causes a lot of environmental damages in addition to consuming nonrenewable resources.

Even though there are various methods and approaches to achieve sustainable architecture, the intelligent integration of traditional and contemporary architecture could be the most promising approach because of its dual roots in past and present. Such an approach would benefit from the best characteristics of traditional and modern architecture. When main considering aspects are on human being and his/her need, responsive architecture to social and cultural context, climate and regional issues, then traditional architecture and urbanism has a lot to offer, whereas when technology, quality and quantity of implementation, quality of life, comfort and environmental issues are the main aspects, then modern and contemporary architecture would be considered as the main sources of solutions.

Sustainability is an umbrella covering many issues and aspects, but none of them are as important as energy efficiency, cost efficiency, ecology and social aspects. Among them, energy is the key item, for energy consumption of buildings could have an impact on environment more than others.

Approximately, construction and building industry use 48% of energy consumption, where 8% is used for construction and 40% for the operation of buildings. As mostly this energy is derived from fossil sources, the result is producing carbon dioxide which is the main cause of global warming (Buildings and Climate Change, 2007).

As in one hand conventional architecture and designs are strongly energy consuming and on other hand, there are available sustainable methods to design and build buildings that can consume up to 80% less energy, architecture and building industry has a huge capacity to address problems such as global warming[1].

Therefore, addressing fore mentioned aspects through promoting energy, resources, cost efficient measures and environmentally friendly solutions are the main objectives of environmentally responsive architecture and construction approaches.

The main considerations regarding such approaches are as follows:
- Selecting sites with paying attention to the environmental impacts.
- Benefiting from renewable energy resources and efficient energy use as the main objective of planning and as a model for energy consumption.
- Water consumption efficiency and effective water conservation measures.
- Waste water management as a tool for efficient water consumption.
- Waste and recycling managements for better use of building materials and components and reducing wastes.
- Indoor air quality management to apply efficient ventilation.
- Outdoor comfort management in sub-neighborhood level for positive influences of open spaces on facades and buildings.
- Material selection considering waste, recycling and energy efficiency issues.
- Architectural outlines considering structural and construction energy efficiency issues.

1 Guideline for Integrated Planning Team

Sustainable guideline consists of series of documents that are actually getting prepared parallel with design process for all team members involving in development, design and construction of building from different aspects. It provides guidance for integrating sustainability during all process of design and construction, it will begin with the planning process and will continue through the construction process, material selection and operation phase and will end with dismantling (demolition) phase of buildings.

The main purpose of this guideline and those who are addressed could be described as:

- Set forth a specific planning and design process for designing and constructing residential buildings, regarding sustainable principles including energy use reduction, indoor environmental quality, water quality and also site preservation.
- Guide the planners, designers, contractors, construction managers, building professionals and workers, and also tenants.

The scope of guideline includes building design-development process, building envelope, interior functions, structural design, site selection, material selection and finally construction process. The provided guideline will cover the entire design and construction process, from early planning phase to the operation and maintenance phase. The guideline provides specific guidance regarding the "how-to" in implementing building sustainability through detailed information necessary for design, construction, operation and maintenance of a residential building. A guidance on how to have less impact on environment whereas cost efficiency, resource efficiency and energy efficiency are the key factors. Among various approaches to sustainability, those including passive design (architectural) strategies are among the most promising ones.

2 Definition and Motivation

Guideline for Sustainable Energy Efficient Architecture & Construction is an approach to provide a manual for creating sustainable architecture and structures and at the same time introducing procedures that are environmentally responsible and resource-efficient throughout a building's life cycle from site selection to design, construction, operation, maintenance, renovation and demolition of buildings, as complementary principles for classical building designs consisted of economy, utility, durability and comfort.

2.1 Environmental Impact of Convenience Approach
Sustainable architecture and construction guideline is an environmentally strategic approach to address unaware consumption of "energy, water, materials and other natural resources" during various stages of "site selecting, designing, constructing, operating, maintaining, renovating and demolishing". When "environmental effects are taking place, damages and impacts are such as:

- Over exceeding in non-renew able energy consumption.
- Over exceeding in producing waste.
- Overall damage on environment.
- Social problems related to inappropriate designed architecture and construction.
- Economic problems related to inappropriate designed architecture and construction.
- Serious health problems of citizens.
- Air pollutions.
- Water pollutions.
- Indoor pollutions.
- Heat islands phenomenon.
- Drinking water and storm-water runoff.

2.2 Benefits of Applying the Guideline
Application of sustainable architecture and construction guideline could result in lots benefits from different aspects:

Environmental aspects
- Reducing negative Impacts on natural environment.
- Reducing waste.
- Spreading recycling culture.
- Enhancing protection of biodiversity and ecosystems.
- Protecting natural environment.
- Selecting sites, materials and construction methods with environmental awareness.

Economical aspects
- Reducing running and operation costs.
- Reducing overall life cycle costs.
- Reducing maintenance costs.
- Increasing use of more sustainable materials and elements.
- Social aspects.
- Increasing indoor and outdoor comfort.
- Optimizing quality of life.
- Approving aesthetic qualities.
- Increasing social connections by affecting sense of belonging.
- Increasing sense of satisfaction.

Energy aspects
- Reducing home energy consumption and increasing proportion of renewable energy consumption.
- Reducing home water consumption and managing waste water.
- Awareness in selecting materials with less gray & embodied energy.
- Awareness in selecting materials with less CO_2 equivalent.
- Reducing waste production throughout the procedure of construction and life cycle of house while spreading out recycling culture.

---

[1] Zero energy buildings could be mentioned as example

II
Sustainable Design Strategies

Sustainable Design Strategies

Procedure of sustainable design introduces the methods to develop energy efficient and environmentally sensitive buildings. Such methods demonstrate how to design, develop and construct all buildings in general and residential buildings in particular, in order to:
- Minimize the environmental impacts of new buildings.
- Maximize use of renewable resources in the created building environment.
- Minimize energy and water use and negative environmental impacts of new buildings.
- Improve overall health, comfort and productivity of occupants.
- Improve energy consumption patterns.
- Minimize resource consumption.
- Reduce life cycle costs.
- Improve context responsivity of buildings.

Among various approaches towards sustainability, "passive solar strategies" are well known due to cost efficiency and context friendliness of its principles and measures.

The approach of architectural passive design strategies could be considered as the most applicable approach for resource saving and sustainable architecture and construction, considering special situation of Iran in particular and MENA region in general.

Such an approach requires paying special attention to climate, social characteristics of current or prospective inhabitants, topographical-physical characteristics as well as architectural characteristics of the understudied area. The relationship and interactions among society, building and its architecture and climate is "site-specific" and dynamic, therefore should be studied and analyzed properly throughout the specific project process for each certain place. The most expecting outcomes are precise definition of passive design strategies generally for residential buildings in MENA region and specially for Iran.

Consideration of above mentioned items and applying the suggested strategies will obviously lead to higher levels of thermal comfort and cost efficiency while reducing energy consumption, life cycle cost of building, and CO_2 emission through energy efficiency by applying passive measures and resource saving design.

The most effective strategies with low initial costs and long term savings in operational costs could be listed as:
- Proper orientation.
- Proper elongation.
- Proper form and layout.
- Proper window positioning.
- Proper opening to wall ratio.
- Proper massing for the walls.
- Proper zoning and placement inside the building (locating different spaces according to function and time of use).
- Proper materials.
- Proper structural system.
- Proper workmanship.

1 Basic Terms and Definitions

1.1 Climate and Thermal Comfort

Passive solar approach, as mentioned before, requires paying special attention to climate and accordingly to thermal comfort.

Climate
Four important elements of climate, affecting thermal comfort and passive design strategies are:
- Temperature.
- Solar radiation.
- Relative humidity.
- Wind movement.

Thermal comfort
To a large extent, thermal comfort is depended on a balance between several ways of giving and receiving heat, such as:
- Heat produced by human body.
- Heat and radiation received by human body.
- Heat lost from human body to the surrounding environment through radiation convention, evaporation and sometimes conduction.

This balance is a necessary condition for thermal comfort. There are various items related to social, cultural and physical characteristics of residents and activities which are affecting the perception of thermal comfort, such as: type and degree of activities, age, clothing, culture and human acclimatization (Climate and Comfort-UNDP, 2005).

The above mentioned items are divided in two categories as "environmental determinants" and "personal determinants".

Environmental determinants
- Dry bulb temperature.
- Relative humidity.
- Air movement.
- Mean radiant temperature.

Personal determinants
- Activities.
- Clothing.

Very often, dry bulb temperature and relative humidity are considered as the main determinants that define comfort zone which leads to the definition of passive strategies.

The personal determinants could be considered as cultural and local characteristics and could be defined according to local conditions. Other personal factors related to adaptation and acclimatization has proven to affect thermal sensation (Ghazizadeh et al., 2010). As an example for country like Iran, the women's clothing is quite different in compare with western style of clothing; therefore it is necessary to use local parameters regarding clothing (Climate and Comfort-UNDP, 2005 & Monam Alireza, 2011).

1.2 Relations between Outdoor and Indoor Comfort
When the monthly outdoor temperatures and the corresponding relative humidity fall outside the comfort zone, introduction of passive strategies helps in maintaining a comfortable indoor environment. The possible situations are as follows:
1. Both main outdoor determinations are within comfort zone; that means a person would feel comfortable outdoors, as well as in an indoor space open to the outside.
2. Both main outdoor determinations are not within comfort zone; that means a person would feel uncomfortable outdoors, as well as in an indoor environment open to the outside.
   In this case, due to the effect of passive strategies, a person inside a building designed with passive strategies would feel more comfortable than a person outdoors.

Perception of indoor comfort
The resultant temperature that affects ones perception of comfort is a function of numerous varying parameters that interact dynamically throughout day, week, month and year (Climate and Comfort-UNDP, 2005 & Monam, Alireza, 2011). These parameters include:
- Internal heat gain.
- Solar gain.
- Relative humidity.
- Ventilation.
- Infiltration.
- Occupants.
- Thermal transmittance (U-value).
- Area and quality of glazing.
- Internal surface temperature.
- Admittance (thermal mass).
- External temperature.
- Internal temperature.

1.3 Relation between Climate and Building
1.3.1 Building Massing
Climatic characteristics should be considered during the process of designing a building, based on contextual approach. The two main important issues are: a building's mass and building's skin. Therefore, it is necessary to analyze the interactions between two important climatic parameters of "solar radiation" and "air movement" with building's mass

and building's skin. The term "massing" means, the general shape or shapes of a building.

1.3.2 Form and Solar Radiation
The three dimensional aspect of buildings has different consequences on its behavior when is examined with respect to sun and wind alterations (Markus, T., Morris, E., Buildings, Climate and Energy, 1980).

The inclination of roof and walls with respect to the angle of the incident sun rays, determines the quantity of solar radiation reaching the buildings. These considerations have a direct effect on the shape of a building, depending on its context and on the passive strategies that are considered.

Depending on the climate region, this free source of energy can be useful in winter, while its effect can be reduced in summer.

1.3.3 Form and Air Movement
The shape, position and relation of the building to the prevailing wind direction can enhance natural ventilation during summer and mid-seasons by modifying the wind movement in the vicinity of the building.

Shapes, forms and dimensions of roofs and openings of a building can influence the air movement as well. They can create more aerodynamic effects by increasing the airspeed and creating pressure difference. This pressure difference between opposite façades is an effective way to enhance natural ventilation and increase the thermal comfort in summer.

The topology of the site has an impact on the wind speed. If the building is situated on windward side of a slope, the wind velocity over the building will be greater. If the building is situated on leeward side of a slope, a wind shadow will be created, resulting in reduced wind velocity (Climate and Comfort-UNDP, 2005).

1.3.4 Building Envelope
This term is often used in the building industry, and especially when dealing with passive design. It is used very often to describe roof, walls (external and internal), windows and floor of a house. The performance of the envelope is a very important part of the passive design, as it is the main barrier between the outdoor climate and indoor environment.

The function of the envelope of a building is to improve comfort conditions in the interior environment by protecting it from heat and controlling, light, sound, ventilation and air quality.

1.3.5 Building Envelope and Solar Radiation
Through solar radiation, buildings could gain or lose heat through their envelopes, especially roof, walls, and openings as follows:

Roof
Roof is the component that is the most exposed element to solar radiation. Therefore, its protection from sun rays during summer to minimize heat

gain, and its exposure to sun rays in winter to maximize heat gain, are issues to be addressed during successful design stages.

Walls
Walls provide protection from elements such as heat, rain, wind and dust. Depending on the orientation of walls, the exposure to solar radiation varies considerably.

The openings
In general, heat is transmitted through windows at a higher rate than through opaque wall components. This depends on the quality of glazing and the infiltration through the joints. The window size, glazing (with appropriate U-value), shading efficiency and adequate shading devices affect heat transmission and air infiltration.

1.3.6 Building Envelope and Wind Movement
Natural air movement in buildings relies substantially on the building envelope. Some key issues to consider addressing this point are internal air hygiene and correct amount of ventilation needed per season.

In general, cross ventilation can provide easily natural air movements. This would require openings on opposite sides of a space (Climate and Comfort-UNDP, 2005).

2 Principles

"Passive solar design" stands for the use of solar energy to provide heating, cooling and lighting to living spaces.

Passive solar design is applied in several countries across the world and has proved to produce houses which energy efficient (and consequently low running costs), need less maintenance, and are comfortable and healthy to occupy.

As a general design approach, the key considerations with respect to passive design are determined by the geographical and climatic characteristics of context. There are various passive solar design techniques which have been used around the world. However, it is essential that the used passive design techniques, are beneficial and applicable in the climate framework where the house is located.

As a matter of fact, a building design according to the passive principles must have closer relationship with surroundings (much more than a conventional building design) to achieve a comfortable internal environment with a minimum amount of resource use.

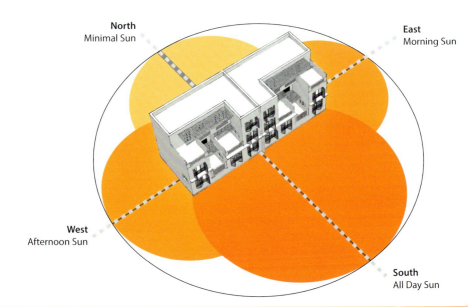

Fig. 1: Solar radiation in different orientations

2.1 Orientation
Good orientation increase the energy efficiency of a house, making it more comfortable to live in and cheaper to run.

2.1.1 General Principles
Orientation refers to the azimuth angle of a surface, relative to true north. With regards to building design, orientation of a building can significant-

ly affect its potential to capture prevailing breezes and its exposure to solar radiation. The density of solar radiation varies depending on the orientation. It is therefore a very important first step towards applying good passive design strategies.

An effective passive solar design should assume that the building is oriented to receive direct solar radiation the most in winter (when heating is the main issue) and much less in summer (when cooling is the main issue) (see Fig. 1).

Good orientation for passive heating, cooling and lighting ensures the optimum sun radiation from south, east, west, and north and excludes cold unwanted winds during winter and cold months; while ensures cooling breezes and optimum sun radiation for lighting and excludes unwanted sun and hot winds during Summer and hot months.

Good orientation of a house is a very important initial decision and can greatly influence the solar heat gains and loss of the house.

Due to its latitude, the sun altitude in Tehran is high in summer, as shown in Figure 2.

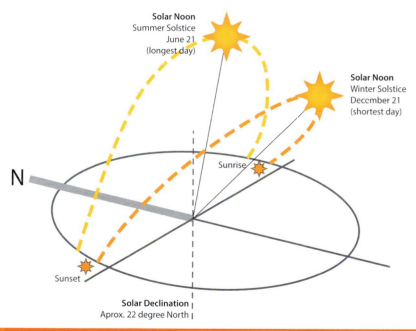

Fig. 2: Solar altitude of Tehran

The image above shows that the sun's altitude is high in summer, when the solar radiation is at its strongest. Therefore, orientating the longest façade of the house towards the south, makes it much easier to effectively apply passive design strategies.

Windows on the south-facing façade can be more easily shaded using extending overhangs to block the high angle sun. The east and west facing façades, however, are subject to direct solar radiation in the morning and afternoon. This factor should be considered in designing functional layout of house (Özsen, 2010 & eCubed Building Workshop Ltd, 2008).

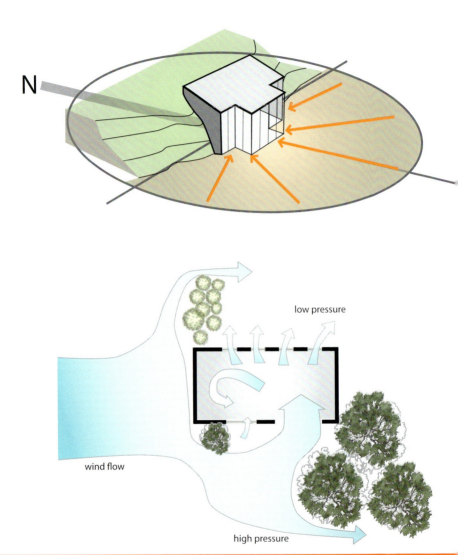

Fig. 3: Maximizing glazing on south orientation and using benefits of a sloped site for shading façades exposed to direct sun
Fig. 4: Example use of landscape to control flow of wind into a house

2.1.2 Design Strategies for Choosing a Site
Selecting a new building site, it is important when the site has good access to sun radiation and cooling breezes. Surrounding landscape and adjacent buildings should not block access to beneficial sun radiation and breezes. If feasible, select a site that would allow optimal orientation of the residential building, in terms of access to sun radiation, wind and shading potential.

A site that contains a south-facing slope can provide beneficial shade to the house. For instance, the south is ideal for location of large windows, as south facing windows require only minimal shading from direct sun.

Solar access however, is also beneficial, as an example, for solar water heaters, clothes drying, and gardens. Therefore, when placing a building on a site (see Fig. 3), solar access should be considered where it is beneficial.

Sometimes, sites with poor orientation, with no access to south sun radiation, or with no access to cooling breezes have to be selected by default. In these cases, an energy-efficient residential building can still be achieved by applying good design principles. For example, high level windows or vents can aid the formation of convective currents for cooling, and letting light in.

The building shape and the landscape around it can also be designed in a way to control the overheating, unwanted wind in winter or unwanted sun in summer (Özsen, 2010 & eCubed Building Workshop Ltd, 2008) (see Fig. 4).

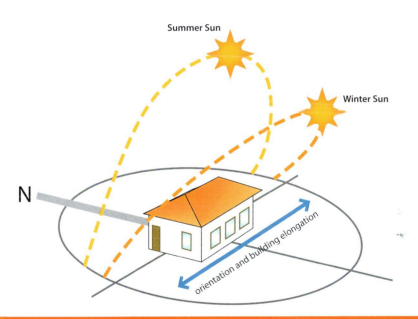

Fig. 5: Proper building orientation on north-south and building elongation on east-west axis

2.1.3 Design Strategies for Optimal Orientation

In regard to passive solar design, for optimal house orientation, the east and west façades should be as small as possible, and have either no windows or very small ones. Rooms which face east and west can also be designed to be used as storage areas, or areas which are not often occupied. It should be considered that long walls in general and not properly shaded opening in particular, on the west or east sides of the building could lead to overheating problems.

Figure 5 shows a residential building with its longer façades facing south, and the smaller façades facing east and west, in order to minimize over heating in hot days.

On a south-facing wall, the sun can be quite easily blocked using eaves (roof overhangs), as the sun altitude is high. However, when the sun is lower in the sky in the morning and afternoon, overhangs will not be effective to protect the east and west facing walls (see Fig. 6).

East and west walls and windows can be shaded using plants and high trees and by using vertical shadings on windows.

Green canopies can also be used as shadings on west and east façades (Özsen, 2010 & eCubed Building Workshop Ltd, 2008) (see Fig. 7).

2.2 Daylighting

Daylight design is the use of light from the sun and sky to complement or replace artificial light (O'Connor et al. 1997). Daylight consists of three components:
- Direct light from the sun.
- Diffuse sky components or daylight scattered in the atmosphere.
- Daylight reflected from surrounding surfaces, such as buildings and the ground.

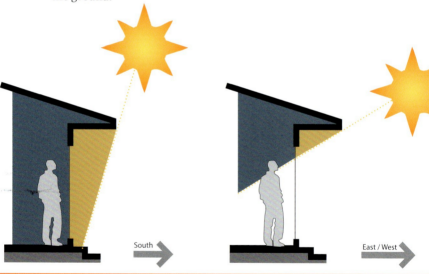

Fig. 6: Effectiveness of shading by overhangs

Daylight is generally preferred above artificial lighting. It is free, has perfect color rendering and a positive effect on human well-being (International Energy Agency, 2001). Vernacular architecture has linked good daylighting with higher indoor comfort and caused satisfaction especially in residential houses.

Passive daylighting systems use windows and shading or redirecting devices to enhance the quality and performance of daylight in a space.

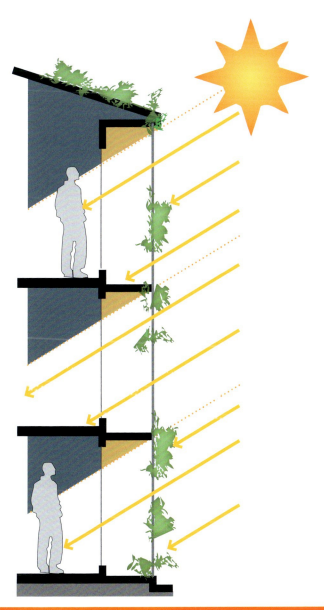

Fig. 7: Effectiveness of using plants for shading

Very often, decisions made in the early design stage could result in efficient and successful design. Appropriate window products and lighting controls are used to optimize daylight performance and to reduce electric lighting needs, while meeting the occupant lighting quality and quantity requirements (O'Connor et al, 1997). As the artificial lighting (and its associated requirement for cooling energy), leads to a significantly higher percentage of energy consumption; daylighting is the most cost-effective strategy to drastically reduce the amount of energy used for lighting.

Controlling the heat gains from direct sunlight transmitted into the space during hot months could prevent overheating through sunlight. Therefore, it is necessary to optimize daylighting strategies to reduce artificial light at most (eCubed Building Workshop Ltd, 2008).

2.2.1 Design Strategies

Daylighting has the potential to significantly improve life cycle cost, increase user productivity, reduce emissions, and reduce operating costs.

Good daylighting requires attention to both qualitative and quantitative aspects of design. The optimal combination of natural and artificial sources provides adequate light levels for the required task.

In order to be effective, daylighting must be integrated with electric lighting design. In particular, daylighting must be coupled with efficient electric lighting controls if net energy savings are to be realized.

As part of a daylighting design, use of continuously dimming fixtures controlled by luminous sensors can be considered.

In general, light which reaches in the space indirectly (such as having bounced from a white wall) will provide better lighting quality than light which arrives directly from a natural or artificial source. Therefore it is important to distribute and control daylight as deep as possible into a building interior, to achieve better quality of daylighting.

The aim of an efficient daylighting design is not only to provide illumination levels sufficient for good visual performance, but also to maintain a comfortable and pleasing atmosphere. Glare, or excessive brightness contrast within the field of view, can cause discomfort to occupants, therefore, controlling glare effect is another factor to improve quality of daylighting.

Dull uniformity in lighting can lead to tiredness and creation of unattractive spaces. Some contrast in brightness levels may be desirable in a space for visual effectiveness. Variety of beam of light in a circulation area is an optimal solution to increase visual interest of the building interior (eCubed Building Workshop Ltd, 2008).

2.3 Shading

Solar gains are required to reduce heating loads during winter months, however, too much solar gain can result in uncomfortable internal temperature or increased cooling energy if air conditioning is installed. The shading design needs to find the balance between the two, normally through optimising the shading to eliminate summer sun, while allowing winter sun to pass into the building. To reduce heat gains, external shading devices are the best performing option. internal shading slows heat down reducing peak loads, but still allows the majority of the sun's heat into the space.

2.3.1 Overshadowing

Topography or surrounding buildings may overshadow a site or the building in it. Longitude will also determine the solar angles over the course of a year, which is an important factor in analyzing over shadowing. The solar access of the site can be investigated by using either a computer model of the site and neighborhood or a sun-path diagram. The degree of solar access must always be determined before the design team can select appropriate passive design strategies. Once an overshadowing analysis is completed, the information is used to orientate the building on the site.

2.3.2 Design Strategies

Design teams need to apply the information from the site shading study to the building envelope when considering effects from direct sun.

The optimal angle for the building in the northern hemisphere is very often a direct southern exposure. However, due to site conditions, this may not be always possible.

It is important to remember that the southern façade will often receive the most solar gain during winter, when the low-angle sun penetrates deeper into the space. The eastern and western façades will also receive high heat gain, particularly the west, which can often become superheated by late afternoon sun after a full day of solar gain.

In fact, a building facing about 15 degrees either side of south will receive optimal winter solar heat gain. Whereas a building facing about 30 degrees either side, will receive 15 percent less than optimal direction (Climate and Architecture, Kasamii, Site Solar energy Iran, 2005). During winter months, the building must maximize any solar gain to help heat the building, while in summer months, sun angle is higher so solar gain may need to be controlled, and in some cases mitigated to prevent overheating (Özsen, 2010 & eCubed Building Workshop Ltd, 2008).

2.4 Storing the Sun Energy-Sunspaces

The most common way to store the sun energy is using sunspace adjacent to living rooms. Sunspaces are simply highly glazed rooms, and are otherwise known as sunrooms or conservatories. They are a means of providing additional living area as well as providing a special mechanism for capturing solar energy. Properly operated sunspaces, that are more than half the length of the south face of a well-insulated house, can reduce space heating energy consumptions by as much as 20–30% (in the temperate climate namely; cool winters, warm summers, and frequent rain) and 40–70% in the sub-tropical and maritime. It is, however, a relatively expensive heating system and also requires very proactive operation by the occupants to achieve energy savings (Donn, Grant, 2010).

2.4.1 Design Strategies

For an effective operation, a sunspace should be able to be shut off completely from the main living areas of the house. This is because sunspaces are most effective as solar collectors when they are designed to overheat. The excess heat is then distributed to other rooms. Sunspaces that are designed as effective solar collectors can sometimes get too hot to be used as a normal living space. Because of the high glazing area of sunspaces, they also lose heat quickly when the sun is not shining. This means they can be uncomfortably cold on cold cloudy days and cold nights. Roof glazing of sunspaces can often make overheating worse in summer, and increases heat loss in winter. An optimum sunspace therefore, has a well-insulated roof and large areas of south-facing glazing.

In the breezy times (more moderate climate), the inside-outside transition zone provided by a sunspace can be a useful as extra living area. It should be designed with good thermal storage or the temperature swings will be huge and much of the solar heat gain will be lost back to the outside. A concrete floor or a concrete or brick wall between the sunspace and the living areas of the house will provide that thermal storage if it sits in the sun for the most of the day. A dark color will greatly increase

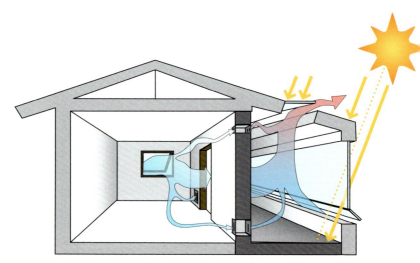

Sunspace principle in summer

Fig. 8: Function of sunspaces in winter and summer

the ability to absorb heat. Colored concrete or a covering such as tiles can achieve this. Openings namely doors and windows, are important for heat distribution. These openings must be to the outside for venting when the sunspace is too hot in summer and to the inside when the sunspace is hot in winter (see Fig. 8).

As sunspaces have such a direct path for heat loss and gain through the glass, they should never be heated. It happens quite easily to consume more than double the whole house heating energy by using a sunspace heater just to take the chill off (Donn, Grant, 2010).

2.5 Thermal Mass and Insulation

The three pillars of passive design are consisted of: thermal mass, thermal insulation and proper glazing. Therefore, the combination of thermal mass, glazing type and design and insulation are very important and their interactions need to be carefully considered to achieve the best result.

Thermal mass, stores heat when there is an excess of passive solar energy and/or internal gain in a building and release the stored heat as the building starts to cool down. Another important function of mass is reducing the extreme swings in peak temperature. Therefore, thermal mass is very often an important measure in a passive solar building to control the temperature variation and to reduce the peak cooling loads.

Thermal insulation, as another important measure, slows the transfer of heat through walls, floors and ceilings, from both directions inside to outside or outside to inside. This leads to drastic reduction of energy costs. On the other hand, through retaining heat during the winter and keeping the building cool during the summer, thermal insulation pro-

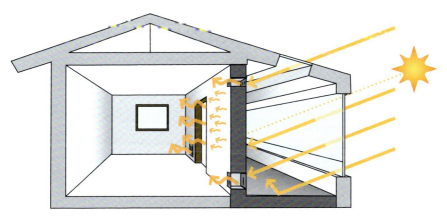

Sunspace principle in winter

vides more uniform temperature inside the building. Thermal insulation in buildings is an important factor in achieving thermal comfort for occupants as well.

The key component of insulation is its R-value (or thermal resistance, the greater the R-value, the better it is at resisting heat movement).

Several types of insulation products exist, including insulation batts and blankets, foam insulation, blown insulation, rigid insulation panels, and insulating materials incorporated into other products such as cladding and structural components (Özsen, 2010 & eCubed Building Workshop Ltd., 2008).

2.5.1 Design Strategies

When conditioning a residential building through passive solar design, the design team needs to understand the close relation between thermal mass and thermal insulation and their interactions with the internal conditions of occupants, functions of spaces and existing furniture inside the space.

The relative positioning of the building's thermal mass and insulation are one of the keys to passive solar design (Hastings, 1994). When a building is categorized as low-gain, mass should be located to receive solar gains from the sun, normally on the floor or as a trombe wall.

When a building is categorized as high internal gain, the mass should be placed away from the sun to prevent the space becoming superheated by the combined effect of mass and the internal gain (The excess heat could be absorbed by exposed ceilings).

Other important considerations which influence thermal mass, thermal insulation and glazing are as follows:

- The building's façade which should be balanced with daylighting requirements which is depended to function of buildings.
- Visible light transmission should be balanced with solar gain and glare effects.
- Even though solar gain is considered always as the free heat from the sun and a key element in passive design, in a high heat-gain building it could be undesirable.
- Glazing areas and types of glass should be optimized for façades. According the orientation they vary.
- Ideally, insulation should be kept separate from the internal environment; as some types of insulation collect dust and can add particulates to the air (Özsen, 2010 & eCubed Building Workshop Ltd, 2008 & Scottsdale Green Building Program, 2005).

2.6 Natural Ventilation

A natural ventilation strategy supplies fresh air without mechanical systems, where the main benefits are high fresh air volumes with a reduced energy use for heating, cooling and mechanical ventilation systems.

Studies have linked increased fresh air rates with increased occupant health (Fanger, 2006). Current sustainable building practice is to supply work areas with above-code levels of fresh air. Typical levels are 150 or 200 percent of the minimum Building Code requirement (eCubed Building Workshop Ltd., 2008). It should be mentioned that the Code requirements will vary depending on the type and functions of buildings. In a mechanical system, the increased fresh air rates cause energy penalties, because fresh air should be heated or cooled to provide comfortable conditions inside the building (Özsen, 2010 & eCubed Building Workshop Ltd, 2008 & Scottsdale Green Building Program, 2005).

2.6.1 Design Strategies
Natural ventilation strategies make use of two generators of air movement: the stack (or buoyancy) effect, where heated air rises and wind, which generates air movement through pressure differences across or within a building. The natural ventilation design should take advantage of the fact that heated air will rise through the building. Considering this fact, designer should provide possibility to release the heated air from the building at high levels and then draw fresh air into the building through the façade.

During hot times, comfort can be achieved by using ceiling fans to generate air movement.

The main obstacles for using natural ventilation are as follows:
- Acoustic requirements, which limits the use of opening windows or other ventilation openings.
- Building Code requirements, for smoke extraction (particularly in atriums).

It should be mentioned, that acoustic concerns could be solved by adopting some rules and regulations during site and landscape planning. As an example, it could be solved through landscaping features or optimal placements in sites (Özsen, 2010 & eCubed Building Workshop Ltd., 2008 & Scottsdale Green Building Program, 2005).

2.7 Airtightness
There is a direct link between two topics of airtightness and air leakage or air infiltration. Therefore it would be beneficial to describe infiltration and connection between them as well.

Airtightness refers to leak in building fabric. As a building with good ventilation and airtight design can resist air infiltration while providing fresh air.

Air leakage refers to uncontrolled flow of air through the gaps and cracks in the fabric of buildings. Sometimes it is referred to as air infiltration, exfiltration or draughts. As it is subjected to wind pressure, temperature differences and changes in the weather; consequently it can be considered variable, particularly responding to outside and weather conditions.

Air infiltration causes several problems such as: heat loss, reduction in performance of the installed thermal insulation, poor comfort, poor control and risks to the longevity of the building fabric. Therefore in order to have energy efficient, comfortable, healthy and durable buildings, it is necessary to control air infiltration (Morgan, 2006).

2.7.1 Design Strategies

There is a link between building complexity and energy performance. More complicated designs with more construction joints tend to have more uncontrolled air leakage—technically known as infiltration, which can have a major impact on heating energy requirements. These leaks can happen between two building elements (for example: doors and door frames, windows and window frames), in the construction materials (for example: weatherboard exterior claddings and timber floorboards are inherently leaky) or they can be the result of complexity of the plan itself (for example: corner joints and joints for cladding changes). The main ways to deal with these are:

- Airtightness strategies should be incorporated at every stage of a project, including design, procurement, construction and running stage.
- Simplifying the design to create less potential air leakage positions (e.g. fewer corners).
- Taking extra care during all stages of project to ensure effective sealing against air leakage.
- Using external wind breaks to reduce the impact of wind on the building.
- Where design and construction still allow possible air leakage, airtightness barriers could be used (Morgan, 2006 & Donn, Thomas, 2010).

2.2.8 Computer Simulation Tools

Using computer modeling to predict the daylighting and thermal or energy performance of buildings is becoming increasingly prevalent, particularly with the introduction of international and national rating systems.

Modeling and building simulation are best used throughout the design process as tools to compare and optimize different design strategies (for example: effect of neighboring buildings on indoor and outdoor thermal comfort, building heights, windows size, placement of openings, glazing type, arrangement of thermal mass and insulation, form and location of plants and greens).

Good passive solar design depends on the complex interactions of several aspects of a building's design. Computer modeling can help designers deal effectively with the complexity of these passive solar design issues, identify and resolve problems of comfort, building performance and energy use, and analyze and fine-tune the design. This accelerates the design process by quickly identifying problems and opportunities, and narrows the range of practical solutions, saving time and money for both design team and client.

In general, a building simulation package should contain the following information:

- Building description: size, shape, and orientation of building, types, sizes, and orientation of windows, construction material types and

their physical properties (e.g. thermal conductance, density and reflectance).
- Design data: insulation levels, internal gain from lights, small power and occupants, infiltration and ventilation rates, equipment efficiencies and desired temperature set points.
- Site data: sky information, weather data files.

The value of computer simulations for achieving a high-quality building, with potential for significant energy savings, is becoming well established. Properly incorporating simulations into the design process can save the design team time and money, improve client satisfaction, suggest energy opportunities that might otherwise be overlooked, and solve problems that could be difficult and include a cost to change while they are still on the drawing board instead of built into a building (eCubed Building Workshop Ltd., 2008).

III
Sustainable Construction

Sustainable Construction

Construction has huge impacts on work and life of society. It affects the nature, function and appearance of cities in which we live and work.

Sustainable construction guideline is an environmentally strategic approach to address anticipated impacts of process of construction on environment. Considering the high amount of construction in Iran, it will be essential for constructors and developers to build in a way that has less impact on local and global environment by adopting sustainable construction measures and strategies.

To address sustainable construction following issues should be considered:

- Site-Environment.
- Initial, embodied and demand energy of materials as well as energy system of building.
- Waste.
- Water.
- Re-usability and recyclability.
- Durability.
- Materials and local products.
- Construction systems.

Sustainable construction
Sustainable construction could be defined as "the creation and responsible management of a healthy built environment based on resource efficient and ecological principles".

Sustainable construction is generally used to describe the application of sustainable development to the construction industry.

Construction industry
Construction industry is defined as all who produce, develop, plan, design, build, alter, or maintain the built environment, and includes building material suppliers and manufacturers as well as clients, end users and occupiers.

Therefore, sustainable construction could be best described as a subset of sustainable development, which encircles matters such as tendering, site planning and organization, material selection, recycling, and waste minimization.

1 Main Pillars of Sustainable Construction

Generally, buildings and process of construction have tremendous impacts on environment; both during construction and throughout their operation. Considering these impacts and as a sign of reflection to them, terms such as: "design green buildings", "build green buildings", "choose green", "environmentally friendly" and "ecological and sustainable materials" have gotten more importance among the terms common in construction industry (Cambridgeshire Horizons & Cambridgeshire County Council, 2006).

Most important issues could be analyzed as principles of sustainable construction and categorized as main fields of sustainable construction.

Charles J. Kibert from university of Florida proposed six principles for sustainable construction; they come as follows (Miyatake Yasuyoshi, 1996):

- Minimization of resource consumption.
- Maximization of resource reuse.
- Use renewable or recyclable resources.
- Protect the natural environment.
- Create a healthy, non-toxic environment.
- Pursue quality in creating built environment.

Due to the nature of construction, how to achieve above proposed principles is an important issue. Three suggested ways for such achievements are:

1. Changing the process of creating built environment from linear to cyclical; to realize sustainable construction, the industry must change the processes of creating built environment, from the conventional linear process to a cyclical process (it means changing the construction processes).
2. Restoring damaged and/or polluted environments; here is the arena of environmental engineering and technology in general, where engineering practices for treatments of damaged and contaminated soil, water and air are major examples of activities.
3. Improving arid environments; the civil engineering and construction industry's involvement in the fight against desertification is a straightforward example of activities in this arena.

While all three arenas are important, it is reasonable to pay more attention to the first issue, as main priority: changing engineering and construction processes from linear to cyclical, where following measures should be considered:

- Designing buildings, structures and regional planning with optimum energy efficiency and minimum energy consumption including application of the concept of life-cycle assessment.

- Using environmental friendly materials including recycled materials.
- Developing a construction system that provides lower carbon-dioxide emission and energy consumption.
- Using environmentally clean machinery and equipment.
- Minimizing discharge of waste from "building sites" and providing efficient waste managements.
- Reusing/recycling left over materials as much as possible.
- Minimizing use of timber and woods considering special conditions in Iran.
- Using local materials as much as possible.
- Reducing water consumption during construction process and providing as efficient water management as possible.

At the present time "Environmental-friendly construction method" has turned to be the most promising method of construction, which is established based on four pillars as follows:
1. Construction systems.
2. Building elements.
3. Ecological building materials (Chapter IV).
4. Applicable measures for energy efficiency (Chapter V).

In this chapter and next two chapters, the above four mentioned pillars will be studied and analyzed.

2 Construction Systems

Before deciding on any construction system, for a building project, several factors should be considered. Factors such as:
- To check with the local building department and authorities about the acceptability of systems and materials according to local construction codes.
- To check the possibility of implementation of proposed systems, in case of innovative systems or materials.
- To check the availability of experts and skilled workers who are able to implement proposed systems.
- To check the availability of maintenance and necessary services after running the building.
- To check the compatibility of proposed construction systems with existing materials and necessary accessories in local markets.

The construction systems could be analyzed, based on different factors. The selected factors are as follows:

Build concept, factory production, insulation, wastage, finishes, labor, installation, transport and lifting, services, hydronic cooling/heating and safety (Building System Comparison & Construction Systems Comparison)[1].

The analyzed systems are as follows:
- Conventional system (Reinforced concrete structure with brick infill).
- Conventional system (Reinforced concrete structure with lightweight block infill).
- Conventional system (Steel structure concrete structure with brick infill).
- Conventional system (Steel structure with lightweight block infill).
- Timber frames.
- Conventional panels.
- Lightweight steel frames.
- Precast modular.
- Tunnel forms.

The aforementioned systems can be categorized under six main groups as follows:

2.1 Block Work, Brick Infill

"Block work or brick infill" is a system consisted of separate structures of beams, columns and floor systems with various types of blocks as infill. Sub & super structure formed of reinforced concrete or steel frames with brickwork infill for walls and partitions with plaster finishing.

Characteristics of block work, brick fill system

Description, building concept	•• Requires separate structures of beams, columns and floor systems using precast •• Wall in-fills need more jointing details •• Must use separate floor systems for multi-levels
Factory production	•• More on-site trades: reinforcement, steel frames, bricks or blocks laying and rendering •• On-site labor intensive •• Load-bearings need to be steel and reinforced concrete •• Concrete pump and untidy •• Steel welding or screw, untidy
Insulation	•• N/A
Wastage	•• Excessive site wastage, cleanup, disposal: cutting of bricks and blocks, pallets, mortar, sand piles, hoses and water
Finishes	•• Only achieved by site application, increased labor costs and inferior accuracy •• Colored bricks available but generally need to apply another finishing or lining
Labor	•• Labor intensive •• Requires more site amenities, supervision, temporary services and scaffolding
Installation	•• Slow •• Labor intensive •• Greater overhead costs
Transport and lifting	•• Extensive scaffolding, material hoists and safety provisions
Services	•• Must be progressively manually built in or chased in later
Hydronic cooling/ heating	•• Is possible, but the running costs could be relatively high
Safety	•• Excessive site labor with potentially high injury risks •• Loose power leads, hoses and scaffolding creates safety risks

2.2 Block Work, Lightweight Block Infill

"Block work, lightweight block infill" the same as Block work or brick infill is a system which is consisted of separate structures of beams, columns and floor systems with various types of blocks as infill. Sub & super structure formed of reinforced concrete or steel frames with lightweight block infill for walls and partitions with skim coat/plaster finishing.

Characteristics of block work, lightweight block fill system

Description, building concept	•• Requires separate structures of beams, columns and floor systems using precast •• Wall in-fills need more jointing details •• Must use separate floor systems for multi-levels
Factory production	•• More on-site trades: reinforcement, steel frames, brick or block laying and rendering •• On-site labor intensive •• Load-bearing needs to be steel or reinforced concrete •• Concrete pump and untidy •• Steel welding or screw, untidy
Insulation	•• Different levels of thermal insulation
Wastage	•• Excessive site wastage, cleanup, disposal: cutting of bricks and blocks, pallets, mortar, sand piles, hoses and water
Finishes	•• Only achieved by site application, increased labor costs and inferior accuracy •• Colored bricks available but generally need to apply another finishing or lining
Labor	•• Labor intensive •• Requires more site amenities, supervision, temporary services and scaffolding
Installation	•• Slightly faster construction •• Slightly reduction in labor •• Lower construction costs •• Easy structure convertibility (extension/renovation) •• Fast to skim coat/plaster •• Greater overhead costs

Transport and lifting	•• Extensive scaffolding, material hoists (raising in site) and safety provisions
Services	•• Must be progressively manually built in or chased in later
Hydronic cooling/ heating	•• Is possible, but the running costs could be relatively high
Safety	•• Excessive site labor with potentially high injury risks •• Loose power leads, hoses and scaffolding create safety risks

2.3 Conventional Panels

Panels are flat elements which have been casted on flat table. Conventional panels should be installed individually and required numerous joints, brackets and grouting in site.

Characteristics of conventional panels system

Description, building concept	•• Flat elements cast on flat table and installed individually and require numerous joints, brackets and grouting
Factory production	•• Larger factory area for equivalent production and many more vertical joints
Insulation	•• Must be cast in foam, walls have a perimeter boarder not containing insulation •• Many vertical joints •• Cast in foam layer does not extend to full area of panel
Wastage	•• Minimum 2 layers of reinforcing for insulated walls •• Requires extra 12 m of vertical jointing per room
Finishes	•• Factory painting not possible due to multiple joints •• Color variation as panels are poured separately •• More visible joints

Labor	•• Each panel requires 2 man-days (~ 10 man-days for 5 panels)
Installation	•• Multiple small lifts cause delays, 2 levels per day max. •• 5 crane movements to install 1 panel •• Individual propping and leveling •• Less accuracy with accumulating errors •• No immediate working platform until the jointing is completed
Transport and lifting	•• Needs approximately 8 cranes on site
Services	•• Impractical for factory install windows •• Corner electrical joining impossible •• Plumbing service holes more difficult
Hydronic cooling/heating	•• Difficult/impossible to do with hollow core planks
Safety	•• Installation requires temporary phase (propping) with added safety requirements

2.4 Light Weight Steel Frame

Steel lightweight frame is a light metal element and could be used for cladding the frame gypsum or cement sheet.

Characteristics of light weight steel frame system

Description, building concept	•• Steel lightweight frame, clad with gypsum or cement sheet; many joints to flush fill •• Requires top/bottom elements install first due to tolerances or structure complete for site measure
Factory production	•• Can be panelized but needs to be fixed prior to final cladding •• Access issues for larger premade elements •• Many joints to finish
Insulation	•• Can be placed in wall cavity, or post fixed
Wastage	•• Room sizes not always as per standard steel & cladding sheet lengths
Finishes	•• Much flushing and filling of joints on site •• Pre-painting not usually possible due to multiple joints

Labor	·· Labor intensive to assemble various pieces and several different materials required to complete
Installation	·· Multiple small lifts, 2 levels per day max. ·· Individual piece propping & leveling ·· Post installation access is difficult until floors & other structural elements are completed & cladded
Transport and lifting	·· Can be flat packed; generally lightweight ·· Require site storage areas ·· Difficult to "load" building until all bracing done
Services	·· Impractical for factory install windows; MEP coordination extremely difficult and practically better to do on site
Hydronic cooling/heating	·· Coordination of connections through all the elements generally make it more practical to do in-situ once installed
Safety	·· Significant site labor with potentially high injury risks ·· Loose power leads, hoses and scaffolding create safety risks

2.5 Tunnel Form Structural System

RC Tunnel-form structural system (i.e. box systems), having a load-carrying mechanism only composed of reinforced concrete (RC), shear walls and slabs.

Characteristics of tunnel form structural system

Description, building concept	·· A load-carrying mechanism only composed of reinforced concrete (RC) shear walls and slabs ·· Cast in-situ reinforced concrete shear walls as external walls and party walls with bricks, sand/cement brick internal partitions ·· Cast complete rooms in one piece and install with a single lift ·· Sub-terrain structure ·· Tunnel-form structure provides enhanced earthquake resistance

Factory production	• Monolithic cast of units • No brackets, proper or vertical joints required • Customizable for penetrations and openings • Repetitious production of a module
Insulation	• Precise joints reducing possibility of air transfer • Due to high thermal transmission, using external insulation is necessary
Wastage	• Walls and roofs act together structurally, minimizing the volume of concrete, steel and reinforcing bars leading to less wastage
Finishes	• A nice concrete surface that eliminates finishing works like plastering • Internal and external paint can be applied in the production after installation
Labor	• Installation does not requires skilled workers for plaster coating • Substantial saving in labor
Installation	• Fast to build • Heavy foundation • Heavy lifting equipment required • High thermal transmission • Due to solid, strong monolithic structure, can be 40 or more story in height • The accuracy of the system suits the installation of prefabricated elements, such as cladding panels and bathroom pods • Greater accuracy, monolithic construction reduces bracket and joint costs • Monolithic structure eliminates leakage problems at the joints • Suitable for quick mass housing programs
Transport and lifting	• Heavy lifting equipment required
Services	• Window and door frames, electrical and plumbing conduits can be preinstalled before the concrete is poured • Other facilities such as bathroom pods can be installed as completed units using existing access platforms

Hydronic cooling/heating	•• Pipes can be casted into floor for efficient cooling/heating
Safety	•• Modern lifting techniques •• Safe working platforms •• Enhanced safety

2.6 Precast Modular

Cast complete rooms in one piece and install them with a single lift.

Characteristics of precast modular system

Description, building concept	•• A single trade and subcontract package •• Cast complete rooms in one piece and install them with a single lift •• Sub-terrain structure
Factory production	•• Monolithic cast of wall units and ceiling, in between the equivalent of 5 and 14 flat panels •• No brackets, proper or vertical joints required •• Customizable for penetrations and openings •• Repetitious production of a module
Insulation	•• Closed joints reducing possibility of air transfer •• Mould internal foam layer sandwich panels (200–210 mm) •• External UV reflective coating (up to 100%), available in 45 colors
Wastage	•• Walls and roofs act together structurally, minimizing the volume of concrete, steel and reinforcing bars leading to less wastage
Finishes	•• Internal and external paint can be applied in the production process
Labor	•• Hydraulic mould requires 8 men to operate up to 80 m² per 12 hours •• Installation requires 3 people

Installation	•• A single lift •• No propping or leveling, minimal site fittings, brackets and dowels •• Solid working platform immediately available for subsequent levels •• Erect 4-5 levels in one day •• Greater accuracy, monolithic construction reduces bracket and joint costs approximately $ 100 per room
Transport and lifting	•• 1 crane to extract and place for yard and site
Services	•• Window and door frames, electrical and plumbing conduits built into mould •• Can cast holes in roof slabs for vertical plumbing service, running from top to bottom of building
Hydronic cooling/heating	•• Pipes can be casted into floor for efficient cooling/heating
Safety	•• Modern lifting techniques •• Safe working platforms •• Limited access to external surface required

3 Building Elements

When designing a building, after fulfilling basic spatial, environmental and visual requirements, designer group will focus on the process of detailing the fabric of the building. Choosing proper materials and consequently the manner in which they will be put together to form the building elements is another fundamental task for the designer group. Elements such as: foundation, walls, floor, doors, windows and etc. that largely depend upon their properties relative to environmental requirements and their strength.

Therefore, the process of construction involves an accurate understanding of: the nature and characteristics of a number of materials, the methods to process them and form them into building units and components, structural principles, stability and behavior under load, economical condition, availability of materials and etc.

3.1 Foundations and Footings

A foundation is necessary to support the building and the loads within or on the building. The combination of footing and foundation distributes the load on the bearing surface, keeps the building in level and plumb and reduces settling to a minimum. When properly designed, there should be little or no cracking in the foundation and no water leaks.

The footing and foundation should be made of materials that will not fail in the presence of ground or surface water.

3.1.1 Types of Foundations

Foundations may be divided into several categories, each suitable for specific situation. The main types are:
- Continues wall foundations.
- Pier foundations.
- Pad and pole foundations.
- Floating slab or raft foundations.
- Pier and ground-level beam foundations.
- Piles.

3.1.2 Foundation Materials

Foundation materials should be at least as durable as the rest of the structure. Foundations are subject to attack by moisture, rodents, termites and surface water.

As a rule, any foundation should be continued for at least 150 mm above ground level, to properly protect the base of walls from moisture, surface water and etc.

Foundation could be made of: stone, earth, poured concrete, concrete blocks and bricks. Poured concrete is one of the most common and best materials for foundation in Iran.

3.1.3 Poured Concrete
Poured concrete is one of the best foundation materials because it is hard, durable and strong in compression. It is not damaged by moisture and can be made nearly watertight for basement walls. It is easy to cast into unique shapes required for each foundation (Chudley, 1999 & Rural structure, 2011).

3.2 Walls
Walls could be categorized into two types:
- Load-bearing walls that support loads from floors and roofs in addition to their own weight and resist side-pressure from wind and, in some cases, from stored material or objects within the building.
- Non-load-bearing walls that carry no floor or roof loads.

Each type could be further divided into external or enclosing walls and internal dividing walls. The term "partition" is applied to walls, either load-bearing or non-load-bearing, that divide the space within a building into rooms.

Good quality walls provide strength, stability, weather resistance, fire resistance, thermal insulation and also acoustic insulation.

3.2.1 Types of Walls
While there are various ways to construct a wall and many different materials can be used, walls can be divided into four main groups.

Masonry walls
Where the wall is built of individual blocks of materials bonded together with some form of mortar.

A part from certain forms of stone walling, all masonry walls consist of rectangular units built up in horizontal layers (courses). In order to spread the loads and resist overturning and buckling, the units should lay up with mortar in specific patterns.

The materials in the masonry units can be mud or adobe bricks, burnt clay bricks, soil blocks (stabilized or unstabilized), concrete blocks, stone blocks or rubble. Blocks can be solid or hollow.

Several earth-derived products, either air-dried or fired, are reasonable in cost and well suited to the climate of Iran.

Monolithic walls
Monolithic walls are built of a material placed in forms during construction (two common examples are the traditional earth wall and the modern concrete wall). Earth walls are sustainable, durable and cost efficient if placed on a good foundation and protected efficiently from rain.

Frame walls
Frame walls are constructed as a frame of relatively small members. Very often frame walls are made of timbers at close intervals. By facing or sheathing frame walls on one or both sides, they form a load-bearing system. For the covering the frame walls there are various options, among them, off-cuts are relatively low-cost materials for covering.

Membrane walls
Membrane walls are constructed as a sandwich of two thin skins or sheets. Sheets could be made various materials such as: reinforced plastic, metal, asbestos cement or other suitable materials. In order to produce a thin wall element with high strength and low weight, sheets should be bonded to a core of foamed plastic (Chudley, 1999 & Rural structure, 2011).

Factors that determine the type of wall to be used are:
- Available materials at a reasonable cost.
- Availability of skilled workers capable of using the materials in the best way.
- Climate.
- Use of the building and functional requirements.

3.3 Floors

Building floors are combination of materials and applied systems. In its simplest form, it could be built by compacting the soil which is already exists on the site. In more complex form, it could be built as finished hardwood parquet which is relatively attractive and modern.

An optimal combination of floor's materials and performance could offers protection from vermin and rodents, while is dry, durable and easy to clean. Well-built floor could be a valuable asset to a building. The built qualities of floors depend on the function and application of the spaces, for example floors could be designed and built to be: washable, thermally insulated, sloped, completely smooth and leveled or etc.

3.3.1 Types of Floors

Floors could be built at ground level or above the ground level and this mostly depends on the height, function and situation of buildings.

Solid or grade floors
Grade floors or solid floors are built at ground level; on top of the soil.

To protect the building against flooding, the finished level of a solid floor should be at least 150 mm above the outside ground level. Normally before constructing floor slab, the topsoil would be removed and replaced with coarse material.

Due to important characteristics such as durability, hardness and clearness, concrete is the most optimal material for floors. Concrete offers various combinations and mixture which depend on the function, usage and loading type.

Suspended or above-grade floor
Suspended or above-grade floors are built above the ground level. As these types of floors (built from timber or concrete) are supported on joists and beams, they are called "suspended" or "above-grade" floors.

Due to fire resistance and acoustic insulation qualities of concrete floors, they are a better option than timber floors (Chudley, 1999 & Rural structure, 2011).

3.4 Roofs
As roofs are providing protection from rain, sun, wind, heat and cold; they are considered as essential and necessary parts of buildings. The integrity of the roof and its compliance with the rest of the structural system is an important factor for the whole structure of the building. On the other hand, it is very important in making occupants feel safe.

There are various shapes, frames and covering of roofs, depend on the size and function of the building, the availability and cost of materials and finally their anticipated life and appearance. Roofs could be categorized in different ways.

Flat and pitched roofs
A roof will be considered as flat roof, when the outer surface is within 5° of horizontal, and will be considered as pitched roof when roof has a slope of more than 5° in one or more directions.

There are various influential factors on selecting roofs shape such as: climate, design trends, availability and cost of covering materials.

Two-dimensional roof structures
In two-dimensional roof structures, roof has only length and depth, where all forces are resolved within a single vertical plane. Rafters, roof joists and trusses belong to this category. They fulfill only a spanning function.

Three-dimensional structures
In three-dimensional structures, roof has length, depth and also breadth, where forces are resolved in three dimensions within the structure. These forms can fulfill a covering, enclosing and spanning function. Normally they are known as "space structures". Space structures could be built as cylindrical and parabolic shells, shell domes, multi-curved slabs, folded slabs, prismatic shells, grid structures such as space frames, and suspended or tension roof structures.

Long- and short-span roofs

In Long- and short-span roofs category, the major consideration in the design and choice of a roof structure is span. It should be mentioned that functional requirements and cost efficiency have an influential role as well.

Short spans are up to 6–7 m. They can be covered with pitched timber rafters or lightweight trusses, either pitched or flat.

Medium spans are 6–7 up to 16 m. They required truss frames made of timber or steel.

Long spans are more than 16 m. If possible, long spans should be broken into smaller units. Long spans could be covered using girder, space deck or vaulting techniques.

3.4.1 Types of Roofs

According the shapes, there are various types of roofs.

Flat roof

The flat roof has a simple design. It is adequate for large buildings with columns.

For spans up to about 5 m simple beams can be used. Where spans are longer, for adequate support it is necessary to use deep beams, web beams or trusses.

The structure in flat roofs is consisted of the supporting beams, decking, insulation and a waterproof surface.

Mono-pitch roof

In mono-pitch roofs, slope is only in one direction without any ridge. They are recommended for different types of buildings, due to being easy to build and relatively low cost in compare to other types of pitched roof.

The maximum span of mono-pitch roof is around 5 m (with timber members), in case of wider spans, it is necessary to use intermediate supports.

It should be mentioned that in case of wider buildings, roof will have a high front wall. Which in one hand will increases the cost and in other hand will results a high wall which is relatively unprotected by roof overhang.

Double-pitched (gable) roof

A double pitched roof normally has a center ridge with a slope to either side of the building.

Gable roof, with timber rafters, offers a greater free span than a mono-pitch roof (up to 7–8 m). Even though it is possible to use mono-pitched roofs up to 10 m with less cost, due to the inconvenience of many support columns, the gable roofs are more recommendable.

Hip roof
A hip roof has a ridge in the center with four slopes in different directions. Its construction is much more complicated. That is because hip roofs require compound angles to be cut on all of the shortened rafters and provision for deep hip rafters running from the ridge to the wall plate to carry top ends of jack rafters.

Conical roof
The conical roof is a three-dimensional structure which is more often used in rural areas and for either circular or small square buildings like shrines or tombs. A conical roof is easy to construct and it can be built with locally available materials, with relatively low costs (Chudley, 1999 & Rural structure, 2011).

3.5 Doors

Doors are essential elements in buildings to provide easy access, entry and exit to the buildings. As a border between inside and outside, they provide control over those who are allowed to get in or out of the buildings, as well as security and protection from strangers, harsh climate and etc. General characteristics of doors could be explained as follows:

Size
The size of Doors must be of adequate and sufficient according function and use of space where the door is installed. As an example, following regulations are normally recommended as minimum:
- A door of 70 cm wide and 200 cm high for only one person entry.
- Between 100 cm and 150 cm in width and 200 cm of high, for one person who will be carrying loads with both hands, e.g. two buckets.
- Door's height might be increased to 220 cm to be suitable to carry furniture inside buildings.
- Door's height might be increased to 250 cm if head loads will be carried.
- Door's width 120 for entrance and 90 cm for inside doors.

Strength and stability
To provide stable doors which can withstand daily uses in one hand and can be enough strong against intruders, doors might be built out of relatively heavy materials with adequate structure strong against deformation, which will disturb correct functioning of doors. Therefore, doors are consisted of large panels, such as plywood, or designed with powerful, well-secured braces to keep them square, which allows them to swing freely and be closed tightly.

Weather resistance and durability
Considering climate conditions in designing a door and selecting the ade-

quate material are important factors. Therefore, it is recommended to use materials which will not get easily damaged by weathering.

Keeping the door well painted is one measure to increase its durability. To reduce energy consumption and heat loss in cold times, using insulated doors with weather stripping around them will be quite effective.

According to fire protection regulations and function of buildings, "fireproof" doors could be important and obligatory.

3.5.1 Types of Doors
Unframed doors
Unframed doors are very simple doors that could be made from a number of vertical boards. These doors are held securely by horizontal rails and a diagonal brace. Brace should be installed in such a position that keeps it in compression.

Framed doors
Framed doors are more rigid elements, consisted of a frame around the outer edge of the door. This frame is held together at the corners with mortise and tenon joints.

Due to the making inner panels from several boards, it is necessary to use bracing for more durable doors. In case of using one or two panels of plywood, bracing is not required any more.

For large doors of stores and garages, bracing is necessary.

Flush doors
Flush-panel doors are consisted of a skeleton frame and a sheet facing as cladding (as example plywood). Here, bracing is not required.

As advantages of this type of doors: the plain surface is easy to finish, to keep clean and can be insulated easily during the construction process.

Double doors
Double doors are used in case of having large openings. In case of using hinged doors, smaller double doors are much stronger against sagging and bending. In the same way, they are less affected by wind.

Rolling doors
Rolling doors are adequate alternatives to double-hinged doors in case of large openings. Very often rolling doors are mounted under the eave overhang. Even though they require space at the side of the doorway when they are open, but there are various designing options to suit different situations.

They have several advantages such as:
- Operate more easily.
- Are affected less by wind.
- Are subjected less to sagging and warping in compare to swinging doors.
- Are protected better from the weather either open or closed.

Half-door or Dutch door
Half-doors are divided in half horizontally. It is possible to open the top section of half-doors separately. Therefore they let in air and light while preventing the entry or exit of people.

3.5.2 Doors Frames
A simple door frame consists of two side posts or jambs, a sill or a threshold and a head or a soffit. For better controlling the heat loss, a tightly fitting door is needed. Therefore, a complete frame including strips or stops around the sides and top (which the door closes) is required.

To have the door being closed tightly, it is necessary to have a threshold or a head. A threshold allows the door to be closed with a relatively tight fit at the bottom. In the same time it allows the door to swing open with adequate clearance from the floor. The head permits the top of the door to close tightly.

As another important advantage, a door with threshold can provide better insulation from outside weather as well (Chudley, 1999 & Rural structure, 2011).

3.6 Windows
Windows are very important elements at buildings which are providing light, ventilation, view to the surrounding landscape and observation of outside.

It is recommended that for the rooms and work spaces where natural light and ventilation are important, the windows area to be at least 15–25 percent of the floor area of the room.

In regions such as Iran, windows very often need to be shaded to reduce heat radiation in one hand and have the possibility to being closed to keep out driving rain or dust. To protect from insects, screening may be needed.

To provide necessary protection against overheating, shutters (either top- or side-hinged), louvers or etc. are strongly recommended.

Shutters
Shutters are normally small doors which are constructed as unframed, framed or flushed. Due to the size, when it is small, only two rails could be required.

According to the situation, window shutters can be side-hinged or top-hinged. The main advantages of a top-hinged shutter are:
•• Shading the opening when kept open.
•• Allowing ventilation while preventing rain from entering.

The principles of construction of shutters are the same as for doors.

3.6.1 Windows Frames

Windows could be built in a number of different frames. By appropriate combination of windows frames and glazing type, it is possible to improve the thermal resistance of the windows and increase overall energy efficiency, particularly its U-value.

Aluminum or metal frames

Despite of strong, light and easy maintenance metal or aluminum frames, due to high and rapid heat conductivity of them, it is necessary to use thermal break (an insulating plastic strip which should be placed between inside and outside of the frame and sash) to reduce heat flow and improve its U-value.

Composite frames

Composite window frames are consisted of composite wood products, such as particleboard and laminated strand lumber. They are very stable and normally offer better structural and thermal properties and better moisture and decay resistance than conventional wood.

Fiberglass frames

Fiberglass frames are dimensionally stable and have air cavities, which could be filled with insulation. The very reason that can increase their thermal performance in compare with wood or uninsulated vinyl frames.

Vinyl frames

Vinyl frames known as (PVCs) are usually made of polyvinyl chloride with ultraviolet light (UV) stabilizers to keep sunlight from breaking down the material.

Normally they do not need painting and offer good moisture resistance. The hallow cavities of vinyl frames could be filled with insulation materials to strongly increase thermal performance of the frames.

Wood frames

Wood frames offer relatively good insulation properties. They need regular maintenance and due to expand and contract, are subjected to weather conditions (Lawrence Berkeley National Laboratory).

---

[1] References are as follows:
Building System Comparison, *www.duralitegreen.com* & Construction Systems Comparison, *www.aeconline.ae*

IV
Ecological Building Materials

Ecological Building Materials

Understanding the importance of "sustainable or green construction", has made the selection of materials an important issue. Consequently, establishing a reliable set of norms, as guidance for selecting appropriate materials for construction, insulation or finishing is regarded more and more as a basic step in process of sustainable construction. Therefore, in this part of study after adopting sets of criterion, different common materials such as: concrete, timber, aluminum, metal, PVC frame, wooden frame and appropriate materials for finishing will be analyzed and compared[1].

1 Criteria for Selecting Materials

The main criteria for selecting proper building materials include common aspects, such as overall impact on environment throughout the procedure of construction (from the early phase of extracting raw materials to the final phase of demolition the building), natural resources, human health and etc.[2]

Generally speaking, there are no clear lines among materials to categorized one as an ecological and another one as a not ecological one, while a material could shift from the most green to the least due to geographical location, distance from construction site, economic situation, human resources and necessary workmanship for extracting raw materials, implementation and etc. As an example, wood construction in areas covered by forests and wood construction in areas with hazardous situation for forests could be mentioned.

Even though there are no common definitions regarding selecting materials, however, following topics are recognizable in various literature regarding criteria for selecting eco-friendly materials; topics such as: embodied energy, pollution, local production, reusability-recyclability and durability. Therefore considering them as common acceptable basis for evaluation and comparison of different materials is reasonable (Indriksone, Bremere, Aleksejeva, Grätz, Oisalu, Svirskaite, 2009 & Buckley, Halsall).

Embodied energy of common materials
Under this criterion, the energy used to produce a material as well as sources of energy will be addressed. Production and exploitation of construction materials are subjected to energy consumption at various stages. The stages could be listed as from: extraction of raw materials, transportation to factories, manufacturing the materials in factories, energy consumption of factories for running the machines and heating and lighting, transportation of product to sites where construction will take place, maintenance of buildings, demolition of buildings, transporting the construction debris to waste storage areas and finally disposal stages.

Selected data from the Inventory of Carbon and Energy ('ICE') prepared by the University of Bath (UK), (see Fig. 9) and is available at: *http://perigordvacance.typepad.com/files/inventoryofcarbonandenergy.pdf*

Therefore, it is crucial to keep extraction, processing and refining phases of converting raw materials to construction materials as simple as possible. Accordingly, it leads to a less embodied energy level and consequently reduces the related CO_2 emissions.

Pollution and waste

Normally in a conventional building, the selection of materials and making decisions that which materials should be used is based on physical properties, price, and availability of them, which are somehow connected together. Precise information about whole stuff used in the manufacturing process of materials is essential for an ecological evaluation of building materials. It is also important to know how these ingredient materi-

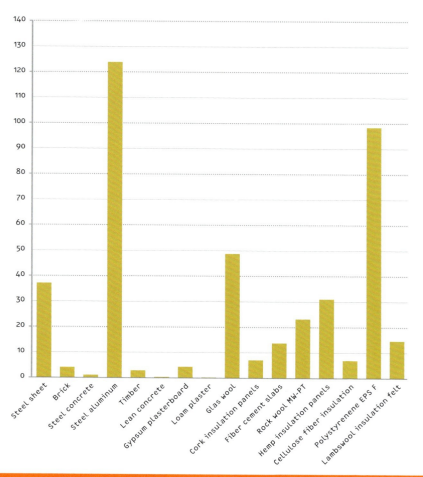

Fig. 9: Values of embodied energy for most common construction materials [MJ/kg]

als are reacting to each other. As normally, health problems are accruing through the emissions of toxics from materials used in the building construction, to have a healthier indoor, it is recommended to use natural materials, which are characterized as having no or the least toxic chemical additives. In the following part some of the most possible emissions and potential materials related to such emissions and their negative effects are listed.

Emission	Materials	Negative effect
Formaldehyde	•• Pressed wood boards (e.g. MDF, OSB) and furniture made of these pressed wood products •• Urea-formaldehyde foam insulation (UFFI)	Eye, nose and throat irritations; wheezing and coughing, fatigue; skin rash and several allergic reactions. May cause cancer
Mineral fiber, dust	•• Insulation and noise prevention materials (mineral wool, perlite)	Eye, nose and throat irritations
Styrene emissions from EPS burning	•• Expanded polystyrene (EPS)	Harmful, toxic by inhalation, irritating to eyes, respiratory system and skin
HCl emissions from PVC burning in cases of fire	•• Polyvinyl chloride (PVC) window frames, linoleums	Causes severe burns to skin, eyes and lungs
Dioxin emissions from PVC burning in case of fire	•• Polyvinyl chloride (PVC) window frames, linoleums	Causes development damages to reproductive, and immune and endocrine systems in very low doses, carcinogenic
Hydrogen cyanide (HCN) emissions from burning of polyurethane in cases of fire	•• Insulation materials-polyurethane (PUR)	Very toxic

There is a possibility to have toxic emissions after the completion of building. As an example, disposing rest of materials (waste) in landfills could be mentioned. Therefore, emissions and their hazardous effects could be reduced by using renewable sources, with more potential for decomposing.

Local production
Providing building materials from local producers has various advantages such as:
•• Reducing transport and the related energy, therefore less emissions, as ecological advantages.
•• Reducing transport related costs, as economic advantages (see Tab. 1).

- Strengthening the local economy by keeping capital in the area and increasing job possibilities, as economic advantages.
- Using local materials increases access to the expertise and support from producers.

Reusability and recyclability
The issue of reusability and recyclability becomes important, considering the fact that every material, during the procedure of production, has resource footprint and pollution footprint. Using recycled materials can drastically reduce these footprints. In other words, an optimal environmental solution for green construction is using the recycled materials, as well as using recyclable materials, where, after demolition of buildings, its materials could be reused. According this criterion, a material that is recyclable is easily preferable to a material that is not recyclable, even when second one can be categorized as a green material.

Durability & interdependency
This criterion is dependent on different items such as: quality of used materials, building type, building design, building function and necessary period of maintenance of building. The key factors here are:
- Durability based on effective life span of product; or the time that certain product should be removed or replaced.
- Durability based on maintenance period of products as the products may have long or short span of life according to frequency of maintenance.
- Durability based on interdependency of system and its different constituting parts, designing the relationship between different elements of system that as a whole can properly function.

Transport Mode	MJ/km
By air	33.0 – 36.0
By road (diesel)	0.8 – 2.2
By rail (diesel)	0.6 – 0.9
By rail (electric)	0.2 – 0.4
By sea	0.3 – 0.9

Tab. 1: Energy consumption in transportation of materials

Considering this criterion in material selection could guaranty the cost efficiency, less energy consumption for new materials and less waste production.

2 Ecological Materials for Sustainable Construction

The main focus here is preparing a system and guidance for finding, comparing and selecting ecological materials for structure and construction. Considering different influential factors on this process, it is necessary to launch an accurate and reliable basis for such comparisons and selections. Therefore selecting influential criterion, from; economical, ecological and technical aspects is getting more important.

Applying such a criterion, on different available and common materials, will assist decision makers to select optimal materials. Accordingly, applied systems will lead to construction procedure with less negative environmental impact, more energy efficiency and in long terms more cost-effective buildings as final outcome.

3 Most Common Constructional Materials

Considering the above mentioned criteria, some of the most common materials have been evaluated from several aspects.

3.1 Concrete

Concrete is one of the most widely used materials for the construction. It is consisted of cement, water and aggregates (gravel sand, rock cuttings, recycled brick gravel). According to the strength demand and requirements, it is possible to use different percentage of mixture of stuff, as well as additives or additional substances. Concrete could be produced in different forms and types, and is categorized as:
- Light-weight or massive concrete.
- Pure concrete or reinforced concrete.
- Reinforced concrete with steel or fibers.

Evaluation of Concrete according main common criteria

Energy	- The burning process of cement requires very high amount of energy
Pollution and waste	- Produced from natural components - High $NO_{(x)}$, CO_2 emission are related to cement production - Pollution of water can occur at every stage of concrete production process
Local production	- Acquired and manufactured locally as there are lots of local producers of cement and concrete - Extraction of raw materials leads to strain on local environment
Reuse and recycle	- Recyclable materials, reinforcing steel and other embedded items, if any, must be removed
Durability and interdependency	- Hard wearing and long lasting, but once it has started cracking or becoming uneven, needs to be replaced or covered with further layers of new concrete - Non-biodegradable

3.2 Timber

Wood is a renewable source but not widely available in Iran. Timber products show a good balance between the strength and weight of the material.

There are several advantages of using timber, especially timber with the FSC6[3] certificate in construction, but several serious negative aspects when selecting timber for construction should be considered, such as scarcity of wood in most part of Iran, dangerous effects of cutting the forest on soil, land, and quality of air and etc.

Evaluation of timber according main common criteria

Energy	•• Timber products mostly have relatively low embodied energy. Industrially processed glued wood requires relatively high embodied energy. Naturally dried wood is preferable in terms of energy consumption and with respect to technical properties
Pollution and waste	•• Might need treatment, impregnation and additives to improve properties (e.g. biodegradation, hygroscopic, fire resistance) in application. Wood products can emit VOCs. Emissions from coated wood types are possible depending on the agent used. Wood protection agents can be avoided if the proper type of wood is selected for specific applications and the wood has been stored and dried properly •• Environmentally friendly surface coatings e.g. oil and wax do not cause harmful emissions •• Noise and dust are workplace hazards •• Treated wood can be disposed of at incineration plants
Local production	•• Renewable, local source, however, intensive wood cutting due to less forest, can cause pressure on the environments
Reuse and recycle	•• Reuse is possible if wood can be dismantled without damage •• Untreated wood can be used as a raw material for a number of applications e.g. cellulose industry or in combustion for energy generation
Durability and interdependency	•• Well suited for prefabricated constructions (carcass, panel houses) •• Durability depends on proper installation, maintenance, treatment and type of wood

3.3 Aluminum (Frame)

Aluminum is mostly used to make frames in construction industry in Iran. Even though it is quite lightweight, conduct heat very rapidly. Therefore, it is recommended to place an insulating plastic strip between the inside and outside of the frame and sash, when energy efficiency is one of the basic considerations.

Evaluation of Aluminum frame according main common criteria

Energy	•• Very large amount of energy is required (very high embodied energy)
Pollution and waste	•• Aluminum industry is one of the greatest sources of fluoride hydrocarbons, e.g. in Germany •• Source of occupational diseases
Local production	•• Non-renewable source •• Although offered on the whole Iran market, is not produced everywhere in the country
Reuse and recycle	•• Recyclable and reusable (if carefully disassembled)
Durability and interdependency	•• Very durable, requires low maintenance •• Contacts between different metals should be avoided in order to prevent materials from corroding

3.4 PVC (Frame)

Another material commonly used as frame is "Polyvinyl chloride (PVC)". PVC is a synthetic material, made of alternating units of vinyl chloride. Due to properties such as: adequate thermal insulation, adequate sound insulation, adequate price in comparison with wooden frames, PVC frames are most favored materials as frames.

Evaluation of PVC frame according main common criteria

Energy	•• High embodied energy
Pollution and waste	•• The polymer itself is not toxic during the use
	•• Dioxins are formed during numerous stages of the vinyl lifecycle, e.g. in production of chlorine, burning of vinyl products in accidental fire. Other pollutants related to PVC are e.g. phthalates, Metals, vinyl chloride. Due to its high pollution load, several countries have imposed restrictions on the use of PVC
	•• Vinyl products are disposed in incinerators or in landfill where they add to the share of long-lasting products
	•• Mechanical recycling can release additives, including phthalates and stabilizers
Local production	•• Non-renewable source
	•• There are growing tendency for installation of PVC frames
Reuse and recycle	•• Because of a great mix of additives, PVC is extremely difficult to recycle. Also the recycled post-consumer product is always of a lower quality than the original material
Durability and interdependency	•• Moderately durable, low maintenance, does not require painting, however if problems with windows frame occur while in use, refurbishment might be complicated. At high temperature may expand and warp: at extremely low temperature may crack
	•• Good moisture resistance
	•• It is important that PVC frames have a good micro-ventilation system built-in in order to reduce water condensation on glass

3.5 Wooden (Frame)

Frames could be built from wood too. Even though wooden frames look friendlier and create more attractive facades for buildings—especially for residential buildings—, due to various factors, they are not recommended strongly. Factors such as: scarcity of wood in most part of Iran, environmental issues related to the shortage of wood and forest, high cost of good quality timber, thicker frame in comparison with aluminum and PVC.

Evaluation of wooden frame according main common criteria

Energy	•• In comparison to metal and PVC frames, they have a relatively low embodied energy, aluminum clad timber frames have a higher embodied energy
Pollution and waste	•• If timber is not FSC certified, the risk for habitat destruction and pollution occurs •• In order to increase their durability, they are most often treated, increasing pollution risks resulting from synthetic based paints (e.g. VOCs, hazardous waste during manufacture, paints are non-biodegradable). Plant based paints should be given preference •• Noise and dust are workplace hazards, and precautions if treating with chemicals should be taken •• Treaded wood is down-recyclable as fuel
Local production	•• Renewable, local source •• Although offered on the different cities in Iran market, is not produced everywhere in country
Reuse and recycle	•• Can be reused, if not chemically treated can be recycled
Durability and interdependency	•• Expansion and contraction according to weather conditions. Frames are less affected by temperature; but can be affected by moisture and thus require the most maintenance (repairing is usually required every 5 years). Composite frames have better moisture and decay resistance •• Easy to repair
	•• Aluminum-clad timber frames are expected to have lifetimes of in excess of 40 years. PVC by comparison is around 25 years

3.6 Metal

Various types of metal are produced and used in different parts of buildings. Most steel sheet products are produced through basic oxygen furnace process, which uses 25–35% old steel to make new steel. Very often, embodied energy of metals is quite high in comparison with other construction materials. Therefore, this criterion is a crucial item in process of selecting materials, when it comes to select elements made of metal.

Evaluation of metal according main common criteria

Energy	•• Very high embodied energy
Pollution and waste	•• Steel production needs high water consumption, and has a sewage hazard risk •• Dust, heavy metals and heat are the main workplace hazards •• Process related emissions result from galvanization •• Additional organic protective coating is often added (e.g. PVC foils, acrylic, resins, polyurethane or epoxy resins)
Local production	•• Non-renewable source •• Although offered in different cities in Iran market, is not produced everywhere in the country
Reuse and recycle	•• Recyclable. Metal parts can have recycled content up to 95%
Durability and interdependency	•• Very durable (> 60 years). Has a very good ability to withstand wide range of weather conditions. Frames have better moisture and decay resistance •• Low maintenance costs •• High fire resistance

4 Finishing Materials

There are several materials used as finishing. Some of them are produced from natural substances. These are different plastering materials (e.g. clay, lime, tadelakt) suitable for outdoor and/or indoor as well as paints (e.g. lime, clay, casein, linseed paints, egg tempera). Hereby, two types of plaster are described.

4.1 Clay Plaster

Clay plaster is a traditional material produced of clay, fine aggregate (sand) and organic fibers. It is a climatic responsive solution for finishing. Due to its various advantages such as: good heat absorption, moisture regulation, pleasant indoor climate creation, availability in different part of Iran and accordingly lower price range, clay plaster could be categorized among optimal materials for finishing. Furthermore, clay plaster could be used with natural clay color or being painted with a natural paint.

Evaluation of clay plaster according main common criteria

Energy	•• Clay plaster has low embodied energy
Pollution and waste	•• Is non-toxic, emission-free and reduces risks for allergies •• There is a small risk of dust inhalation when handling clay plaster in its dry state •• Does not cause irritations in contact with skin •• Simple plasters can be disposed of in the ground
Local production	•• Clay in traditional architecture is among the main construction materials
Reuse and recycle	•• Can be recycled and reused. Only those coating synthetic components or other setting agents cannot be recycled
Durability and interdependency	•• Although clay plaster is not as resistant as other plasters, in domestic applications the dried surface has good resistance to abrasion. Damage can be repaired relatively easily •• Non-combustible
	•• Will deteriorate if applied onto damp backgrounds or if used unprotected in damp environments

4.2 Lime Plaster

Lime plaster is another material adequate for finishing. It is mostly a mixture of lime, sand, smashed limestone and reinforcing fibers combined with different percentages based on demand and location of application. It is applicable on internal surfaces as well as external. Lime plaster has some characteristics with clay in common, such as: regulating the humidity of rooms and stabilizing the room temperature. In addition, as surfaces plastered with lime are antistatic, they are particularly good options for houses of people with allergies.

Evaluation of lime plaster according main common criteria

Energy	·· Lime plaster has high level of embodied energy due to high temperature (~900°C) employed in its manufacture but less than cement (~1200°C). A standard lime mortar has about 60–70% of the embodied energy of a cement mortar. Has ability through carbonation, to re-absorb its own weight in CO_2 (compensating for that given off during burning)
Pollution and waste	·· Frequent handling can cause eczema. Calcium hydrate is irritating to skin, mucous membrane and eyes. Protective precautions should be taken ·· Non-toxic, thus does not contribute to indoor air pollution ·· Disposal is handled at inert material disposal sites
Local production	·· Overharvesting of lime can negatively influence the local environment ·· Lime is among traditional materials
Reuse and recycle	·· Recyclable
Durability and interdependency	·· Can withstand moisture and rain and temperature changes

5 Insulation

As mentioned before, insulation is among the most important measures of sustainable architecture and construction. A proper insulated building needs less energy for keeping the building warm in winter and cool in summer. These in turn, will drastically reduce carbon emissions linked to global climate changes. See Figure 10 for heat conductivity of most common insulation materials.

According to the origin the available insulation materials could be categorized as:
- Mineral.
- Synthetic.
- Renewable.

It should be mentioned that dependent on application, insulation material could be a mixture of two or all three sorts (mineral, synthetic, renewable) of materials. Mixtures of hemp-lime, fibrolite-wood, or wool-cement are some examples of these kinds of insulation. Despite of differences, all three types of insulations are available for roofs, walls and floors.

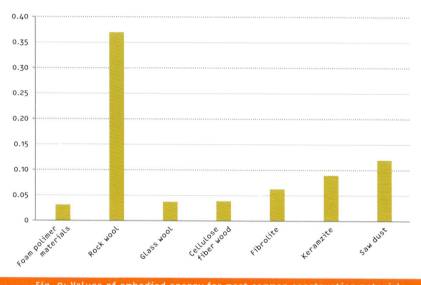

Fig. 9: Values of embodied energy for most common construction materials [MJ/kg]

5.1. Most Common Insulation Materials

Some of the most common insulation materials sorted out based on three categories of mineral, synthetic and renewable materials.

Mineral
- Glass wool.
- Rock wool.
- Expanded clay aggregate (Lightweight Ceramic).

Synthetic
- Expanded Polystyrene (EPS); Extruded Polystyrene(XPS).
- Polyurethane (PUR).
- Polyester.

Renewable
- Cellulose fiber.
- Hemp, flax.
- Straw.
- Wood fiber/wool/shavings.
- Sheep wool.
- Cork.
- Reed.

5.2 Glass Wool

Glass wool is a mixture of sand and waste glass. The insulation is produced by melting the mixture at a temperature >1,300°C. The product is cut and packed in rolls or panels under very high pressure. Due to good thermal and insulation properties, glass wool has a wide range of application in construction.

Evaluation of glass wool according main common criteria

Energy	·· Medium high embodied energy (~50 MG/kg) due to high temperature needed
Pollution and waste	·· Commonly bound 3–9 M% phenol formaldehyde resin for shape retention. Silicon or mineral oil-based hydrophobic agents (~1 M%) are added to increase its resistance to humidity
	·· Glass wool is generally believed to be safe. There is however, a minor risk posed by inhalation of airborne fibers. Some wool has a coating of oil, added to minimize the production of airborne fibers. Airtight construction prevents fine fiber penetration to the air inside
	·· Waste shall be treated as construction waste. Old generation mineral wool considered possibly carcinogenic needs to be dismantled accordingly and disposed of as dangerous waste
Local production	·· Produced in the country
Reuse and recycle	·· Recyclable
Durability and interdependency	·· Very high fire resistance and durability (boards have better shape retention than rolls)
	·· Non-biodegradable

5.3 Rock Wool

Rock wool is consisted of mineral raw materials such as dolomite that are processed into fibers. The final product is produced by melting mineral raw material (e.g. dolomite) together with coke, recycled wool as well as small amounts of lime at ~1,500°C. As mineral wool insulation material is very sensitive to humidity, it should be built under the extreme dry condition. In order to have the best performance, rock wool needs long-term humidity protection.

Evaluation of rock wool according main common criteria

Energy	•• Relatively low embodied energy (~23 MJ/kg)
Pollution and waste	•• Commonly bound with phenol formaldehyde resin for shape retention, silicon or mineral oil-based hydrophobic agents are added to increase its resistance to humidity •• Some migration may be expected during handling (precautionary measures are necessary), but release of fibers after installation is known to be negligible •• Waste can be treated as any other non-hazardous mineral waste and its disposal should be in accordance with national regulations
Local production	•• Produced in the country
Reuse and recycle	•• Reusable and recyclable, can be recovered
Durability and interdependency	•• Very high fire resistance and durability and for at least 50 years in condition of appropriate use •• Non-biodegradable

5.4 Keramzite or Ceramic (Expanded Clay Aggregate)

Keramzite is produced from clay. Clay in form of pellets, is fried at high temperature in a rotating kiln. During this procedure, the organic components in clay will burn off and make the pellets to expand more. The final products (ceramic pellets) could be characterized as light in weight and porous with practically high crushing resistance. Good sound and thermal insulation properties make Keramzite an optimal option for insulation of walls, ceilings and floors.

Evaluation of ceramic (keramzite) according main common criteria

Energy	·· High embodied energy
Pollution and waste	·· Does not contain any harmful substances
Local production	·· Produced in the country
Reuse and recycle	·· Reusable and recyclable
Durability and interdependency	·· Resistant to frost and chemicals, moisture resistant, non-biodegradable, non-combustible

5.5 Foam Polymer Materials (Expanded Polystyrene EPS, Extruded Polystyrene XPS)

Expanded Polystyrene (EPS) is a synthetic product that is mostly consisted of polystyrene. The other materials used in EPS are "pentane, hexabromcyclododecane, dicumyl peroxide and very small amounts of PE waxes, paraffin and metal salts". This product is produced by extrusion. It uses polystyrene granules which are containing a number of additives and with help of foaming agent.

Due to good insulation properties, EPs are strongly recommended. As EP insulation materials are not sensitive to moisture, they can be used for heat and sound isolations in different areas. The product is offered in form of lightweight panels, which makes their application and installation quite easy.

Evaluation of rock wool according main common criteria

Energy	•• High embodied energy (98–104 MJ/kg)
Pollution and waste	•• High amounts of chemicals are required for production •• Hydrocarbon emissions during production process •• EP sheets can emit minor styrene into indoor air even when mounted externally •• Other emissions: pentane, HFC •• Non-biodegradable •• Incineration is only possible in a waste incineration plant, burning releases toxic fumes
Local production	•• Produced in the country
Reuse and recycle	•• Reusable and recyclable
Durability and interdependency	•• Durability >20 years. Durable against weaker acids and alkaline •• Self-extinguishing material in case of fire •• Does not resist aromatic thinners and thinners containing halogens, or other substances e.g. esters, ketones, oils or lubricants. Sunlight can change the quality of the material

5.6 Cellulose

Cellulose is another insulation material belonging to the renewable category. Cellulose is considered among the optimal options as it could be produced from cellulose fibers, such as recycled paper. Cellulose could be produced and used in different forms. As loose fill form, it could be blown into cavity walls, floors and roofs. It could be produced in quilts and boards, which could be installed manually.

Evaluation of cellulose according main common criteria

Energy	·· Low embodied energy (7–18 MJ/kg)
Pollution and waste	·· Boric acid (~12%), borax (7%) are added to protect the material against fire, mould and pests ·· Cellulose fiber dust emissions can occur during blowing in or spraying in process ·· Only borate-free products can be composted instead of incineration
Local production	·· Produced in the country
Reuse and recycle	·· Reusable and recyclable
Durability and interdependency	·· Long life time ~100 years if applied as advised ·· With regard to fire resistance, belongs to the group of hard flammable materials

5.7 Wood Fiber

Wood fiber is a combination of wood wool, cement and water. Wood wool itself is a by-product from the forestry industry. Wood fiber is used very often for insulation of basements, floors and ceilings, as well as sound protection barriers.

Evaluation of wood fiber according main common criteria

Energy	•• Cement components are the main cause of embodied energy
Pollution and waste	•• Does not emit harmful gases, no toxic fumes if burnt •• Safe to work with •• Does not cause problems with waste disposal
Local production	•• Produced in the country
Reuse and recycle	•• Reusable and recyclable
Durability and interdependency	•• Dimensionally stable, high mechanical resistance, UV and moisture resistant, good fire resistance properties •• Not affected by rodents

5.8 Flax and Hemp

This insulation material which belongs to the renewable category, is made out of short fibers of flax or hemp plants. While hemp is a by-product of textile industry, fax is a by-product of linen fiber production also related to textile industry. Very often insulation materials are consisted of both flax and hemp, as well as some materials as binder to support fibers; such as potato starch or synthetic (poly-ethane, polyester). Flax and hemp are mainly good options for wood construction especially for roof insulations.

Evaluation of flax and hemp according main common criteria

Energy	•• Low embodied energy (31–38 MJ/kg)
Pollution and waste	•• Typically contains borates that acts as a fungicide, insecticide and fire retardant. Ammonium polyphosphate or soda are also used as flame protection agents •• Cutting leads to fine dust emissions •• Only borate-free products can be composted instead of incineration
Local production	•• Not produced in the country
Reuse and recycle	•• After renewal of additives, clean material can be re-used
Durability and interdependency	•• No data found

5.9 Sheep Wool

Sheep wool is also categorized as renewable insulation materials. Sheep wool is very especial option due to performing quite well in thermal as well as sound insulation. The product is produced in form of rolls and batts. Sheep wool is a proper option for any type of building and could be used in roofs, walls and floors. Installation of sheep wool is quite similar to conventional insulation batts that make it relatively easy to install.

Evaluation of sheep wool according main common criteria

Energy	·· Very low embodied energy (unless it is imported)
Pollution and waste	·· Usually needs to be treated with chemical (e.g. insecticides), often treated with borax to enhance its fire retardant and pest repellent qualities, synthetic binders might be added
	·· Not irritating to the respiratory system or the skin like fiberglass and other alternative insulating materials
	·· Biodegradable, thus can be composted, if not treated with chemical
Local production	·· Not produced in the country
Reuse and recycle	·· Reusable and recyclable
Durability and interdependency	·· Sheep wool is naturally flame retardant, self-extinguishing
	·· Producers state that insulation maintains its form and will continue to perform for whole life of the building

5.10 Types of Insulation

Insulations are produced in different types and forms.

Different types of insulation

Types	Advantages	Disadvantages
Loose fill-in, blown-in, cellulose	•• Not harmful and fire resistant •• Noise reduction •• Inexpensive •• Thermal and acoustic insulation	•• Absorbs moisture and thus lead to mold formation
Batts and blankets	•• Constitutes of more green and recycled products •• Flexibility of blanket insulation	•• Decrease in insulation efficiency due to the formation of gaps
Rigid board	•• Strengthen the wall •• Effective sound barrier •• Can withstand high temperature •• Fire resistance	•• Installed in open, exposed wall only •• Air and moisture leaks •• Extra costs involved in the long term •• Not flexible
Spray foam	•• Better insulation •• Prevents mold formation •• Long-lasting •• Does not cause irritation •• Ease of installation	•• Expensive •• Messy
Reflective system	•• Prevents downward heat flow	

Loose fill-in, blown-in, cellulose
In this type, insulation is provided from loose and fibrous materials, such as fiberglass, rock-wool and cellulose. Normally, procedure of production of each is as follows:

•• Fiber glass insulation is produced by spinning molten glass into fibers. The used glass is very often recycled glass which is melted in high temperature gas furnaces.
•• Rock wool insulation is produced by spinning from blast furnace slag of rock-like materials. In fact, the procedure of production is as same as fiber glass insulation. The used materials are waste of other productions.

- To produce cellulose insulation, normally recycled newspapers are used. To control health effect they are treated with non-toxic borate.

The advantage of this type is that mostly used materials are waste and recycled. They are normally produced in forms of shreds, granules or nodules. As they are quite small, they are blown to the building cavities and fit well to the spaces where they are used.

Batts and blankets
For producing blanket types of insulation, mineral fibers processed from rock wool or fiber glass are used. They are produced in different widths to fit absolutely between the wood framing members. While the lengths of batts are between 1.2 and 2.4 m, the blankets are offered in longer rolls, which is possible to be cut according the demand length. The R-value of batts and blankets is normally around R-3 per 2.5 cm of thickness.

Rigid board
For higher insulating values, normally rigid boards are used. This type is mostly produced from fiber glass, polystyrene or polyurethane. There are varieties of thicknesses that could fit well to the different situations. The R-values of rigid boards are quiet high as from R-4 to R-8 per 2.5 cm thickness.

Spray foam
The spray insulation types are liquid, containing a polymer material and a foaming agent. The used polymer could be polyurethane or modified urethane.

The insulation is applied by spraying it through a nozzle into the structural element that could be wall, ceiling or floor cavities. After application, it would expand into a solid cellular plastic.

Application of spray foam requires professionals and some special equipment which make it in turn, more expensive.

[1] Based on the report "Using ecological construction materials in the Baltic states" prepared by Daina Indriksone, Ingrida Bremere, Irina Aleksejeva, Matthias Grätz, Sandra Oisalu, Justina Svirskaite within the frame of the project "Using ecological materials in new, energy efficient building in the Baltic states" (2009–11) supported by the German Federal Foundation for the Environment (Deutsche Bundesstiftung Umwelt).

[2] Selected criteria are based on "Using ecological construction materials in Baltic states" & "Considering sustainability the selection of structural system" prepared by Mike Buckley, Robert Halsall, Brennan Vollering and Doug Webber & "Materials and appropriate design strategies for building in hot climates" prepared by Maria V. Machado and Pablo La Roche.

[3] Forest Stewardship Council (FSC) label ensures that the forest products used are from responsibly harvested and verified sources. FSC certification is a voluntary, market-based tool that supports responsible forest management worldwide. FSC certified forest products are verified from the forest of origin through the supply chain (*http://www.fsc.org*).

V
Applicable Measures for Building Physic

Applicable Measures for Building Physic

As mentioned acknowledgment of serious impacts of construction industry on environment, resources and general health issues, has put strong light on topics such as appropriate -construction systems, -construction materials, measure and etc.; when the main approach is described as: environmental friendly construction, sustainable construction, energy efficient construction or green construction.

In this approach, beside prior discussed topics, selecting proper materials and measures has important influence upon overall impact of construction process.

As an example, good passive design simply makes effective use of the sun (and, to a lesser extent, other natural resources such as wind and landscape) to ensure comfortable and energy efficient residential buildings. All buildings -houses makes use of passive solar design to some extent, but not many make very good use of the sun. Providing detailed information on applicable measures and the impact of design decisions should actually help designers and owners to get the most from building designs.

Therefore, based on previous results, some applicable measures such as: appropriate insulations, appropriate glazing, thermal mass, appropriate daylighting, appropriate shading, appropriate ventilations and finally Air- tightness will be studied and considered.

1 Insulation

Insulation is among the most important factors of sustainable approach in general and passive design approach in particular. Due to the dual nature and function of insulation, and its influence on energy efficiency and comfort, appropriate levels of insulation are critical, in both summer and winter. In fact insulation works by controlling the amount and procedure of heat transfer between outside and inside.

1.1 General Principles
Adding insulation to walls, floors, ceilings, roofs and foundations improves their thermal resistance (R-value). The insulation should be properly installed as it contributes to the building's overall energy performance. The building should be properly sealed to reduce air infiltration.

Degree of insulation
According to building codes, there is a minimum, sufficient and maximum level of insulation. Considering importance and influence of insulation on overall energy performance of the building, it is recommended to adopt higher levels of insulations suggested by building codes.

Phase of installing
As it is easier and cheaper to install insulation at the beginning (constructing phase), it is recommended to select higher insulation materials and appropriate installation in construction phase, than later when building is running.

Quality of insulation
Very often the price of higher-performing insulation materials, in comparison with the cost which should be paid for energy consumption of building is less; therefore, it is also recommended to use higher-performing insulation as well.

Adequate installation
Appropriate installation and execution of insulation is a very crucial item in overall energy performance of a building and in adequate function of insulation materials. Here considerable issues are: proper space according to the thickness of materials, adequate bed and cover for insulation materials, installation of insulation without damaging the materials and etc.

Where to locate insulation
Generally placing, insulation in the right position and location has important effects on overall performance of a system. Normally, to create an acceptable bed (hollow space) for insulation, a sub-wall will be framed inside the surface of the concrete blocks. Only after creating this space,

insulation process can be started. As optimal example by using insulation with an R-value of 13 in combination with insulated concrete blocks, will provide a finished wall value about R-23.

Insulated concrete blocks could be applied in different walls of building, which as a result, will reasonably reduce the energy loss of buildings (Donn Michael, Grant Thomas, 2010).

1.2 Design Consideration

The role that insulation plays in the building is determined by its placement. When used in the building envelope, it is preventing heat flow from inside to outside, either containing heat within the building or preventing it from entering. Insulation can be used to isolate thermal mass, shielding the massive elements from unwanted solar gains or shielding occupied areas from the unwanted effects of thermal mass.

It is important to note that any building material has an insulating effect. This is most apparent with floor coverings on concrete slabs. Timber on carpet will effectively insulate the slab and reduce (or eliminate) its effectiveness as a heat sink. Internal strapping and lining to walls will have the same effect, as will acoustic ceiling tiles (Donn, Michael,. Grant, Thomas,. 2010 & Özsen, Emma,. Lee, Tony,. 2010).

The general considerations regarding insulation of building elements could vary based on the elements.

1.2.1 Insulating Concrete Floors

Insulating a floor is an important part of floor heating.[1] Even though extruded polystyrene offers higher insulation values, due to the prices differences, expanded polystyrene is a commonly used material. Optimal thickness is about 15 cm.

To reduce energy wasting and paid money for purchasing energy, it is recommended not to use in-slab electric heating system and floors which are capturing direct solar heat together. It is more effective to combined floor slabs which are capturing direct solar sun with under-flooring heating system that use circulating fluid in pipes buried in concrete floors; as hear, the pipes can distribute heat gained from the sun throughout the building and effectively increase solar gain, which in turn will reduce the purchased energy for heating. The best condition would be a system which can run only in circulation mode without any heated fluid by purchased energy.

Thermal bridge is another important issue which should be considered despite the type of flooring system, while it could drastically reduce effectiveness of insulation systems in general. To avoid thermal bridges, it is necessary to have continues insulation under the slabs and around the perimeters (Donn Michael, Grant Thomas, 2010).

Types of concrete block insulation
There are several common materials for insulation of concrete blocks, such as: polystyrene, poly-isocyanurate, polyiso and polyurethane. The hollow core of block could be filled through pouring, injecting or inserting:
- Loose foam beads.
- Liquid foams.
- Rigid foams.

To provide more structural integrity, one solution would be coating polystyrene beads with a thin film of concrete, which bonds the polystyrene as well. In such a case, used insulation is consisted of expanded polystyrene, Portland cement, sand and chemical additives, which can make a "surface-bonded wall assemblies" with a R-value of R-1 per 25 mm thickness. Using polystyrene inserts in the block cores, will increase the thermal resistance of unit up to R-2 per 25 mm.

The other option would be using a mixture of concrete and wood chips on the hollow core of blocks, which are stacking without any mortar. The stability of the system would be provided by filling concrete and used armatures throughout the wall.[2]

The other option to fill concrete blocks is vermiculite and perlite pellets (Donn Michael, Grant Thomas, 2010).

1.2.2 Insulating Thermal Mass Walls
External insulation
An effective way to provide heat storage is using external thermal walls. Normally, insulation should place on the outside of any wall. By placing insulation inside the wall, it could happen that thermal mass will be isolated from interior part of the building, which also could negatively affect heat storage capabilities of the wall. To avoid this effect, insulation could be fixed to the exterior surface of the concrete wall or, could be placed inside the wall itself but close to the exterior surface. The degree of insulation is depended on thickness of insulation materials and it is adjustable according to ideas of designers. The most common external insulation systems are as follows:
- Placing polystyrene sheets to exterior of walls[3].
- Casting polystyrene sheets into a precast[4].
- Using masonry blocks that are including polystyrene sheets[5].

The important issue with insulation is continuity of the insulation materials. Any breaks could cause considerable inefficacy in insulation systems (Donn Michael, Grant Thomas, 2010).

Internal insulation
There are situations that it is necessary to apply internal insulation and isolate thermal mass. One possible situation is: necessities of fast heat-up

of rooms on north side of building.

In this example, the possible solution is combination of carpeting concrete floor and internally insulating high mass walls.[6]

Some options related to internal insulation could be mentioned as follows:

- Masonry or precast walls, which are strapped with timber and lined with plasterboard, where insulation is placed between strapping to improve energy efficiency of the system.
- Masonry or precast walls with polystyrene boards directly fixed or glued on them. In such a situation, finishing could be applied through plaster systems or plaster boards.
- Insulated concrete formwork-blocks (ICF) (as example polystyrene blocks could be mentioned) which could be filled with ready mixed concrete (Donn Michael, Grant Thomas, 2010).

1.2.3 Roof Insulation

Even though generally it is recommended to use as much as possible insulation; level, location and appropriate materials of insulation of roofs are subject of diverse issues, specially the structure of roofs and used materials.

For a roof with timber-framed structure, where high levels of insulation is demanded, it is recommended to lay down the insulation over the top of ceiling joist. Because there is higher possibility of heat conduction in these points and timber could turn to a thermal bridge.

For the precast and in situ concrete roofs, insulation should be in higher levels, because these types of roofs have a quite good capacity of thermal storage. The same as external insulation of walls, polystyrene sheets could be used. Cladding and drainage are two important issues. Due to lack of access to direct sun, the thermal storage of an internally exposed roof, in compare with a wall or floor, is much less (Donn Michael, Grant Thomas, 2010).

2 Glass and Glazing

Windows are presenting two contradictory aspects. While windows are providing the simplest way to collect heat from sun, they could also be the less insulated elements which can lose the heat and energy the most. Therefore to design optimal windows, which can offer maximum solar gain and minimum energy loss, various factors such as: size, shape, optimal glazing layers, location and orientation of windows should be analyzed and considered.

2.1 General Principles
2.1.1 Orientation
- The longest axis of a house should be oriented east-west to optimize the south-facing exposure.
- Rooms may also be stacked or staggered to achieve a greater south-facing aspect.
- South-facing clerestory windows and skylights can be used to get direct sun into deep plan shapes.

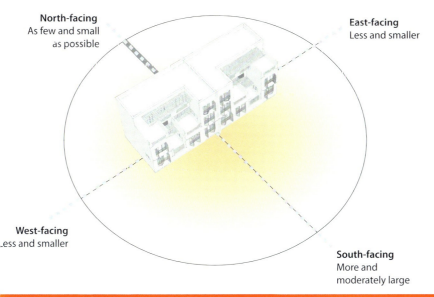

Fig. 11: Guidance for windows orientation

- East- and west-facing windows allow penetration of morning and evening sun that could cause glare and overheating.

    Unobstructed south-facing glazing is best as:
- It captures solar energy in winter (when the sun is low in the sky).
- It is easiest to shade from direct the sun during summer (when the sun is high in the sky) by providing south-facing eaves.

2.1.2 Area of Glass

Area of glass is another determining factor. Even though south, east and west-facing glass are placed to capture solar energy in form of heat and light, inadequate design and size of glass in these positions could lead to the most energy losses as well. Proper designs and dimensions are key factors in energy gain through windows.

As an example, due to the nature of south light, it is recommended to have maximum size of windows in this direction (Donn Michael, Grant Thomas, 2010).

2.1.3 Heat Loss from Glass

As it is obvious that more saving energy and internal comfortable could be achieved through using more energy efficient windows. Nowadays, double glazing windows are more common in Iran especially in Tehran region. Furthermore, double glazing windows can reduces noise transmis-

Glazing Type	U-Factor for Alum. Frames without Thermal Break [Btu/hr-ft^2-°F]	U-Factor for Alum. Frames with Thermal Break [Btu/hr-ft^2-°F]	U-Factor for Wood or Vinyl Frames [Btu/hr-ft^2-°F]
Single Glazing	1.30	1.07	—
Double Glazing 1.27 cm air space	0.81	0.62	0.48
Double Glazing e = 0.20 -1.27 cm air space	0.70	0.52	0.39
Double Glazing e = 0.10 -1.27 cm air space	0.37	0.49	0.67
Double Glazing e = 0.10 -1.27 cm argon space	0.64	0.46	0.34
Triple Glazing e = 0.10 on two panes -1.27 cm argon space	0.53	0.36	0.23
Quadruple Glazing e = 0.10 on two panes 0.635 cm krypton space	—	—	0.22

"e" is "emittance" of the low-E coated surface.

Tab. 2: Influence of frames, glazing panes and spacers on U-Factor (U.S. Department of Energy)

sion through windows and window condensations.

The best performing windows allow less than a half of the heat loss of standard double glazing, and less than a quarter of the heat loss of standard single glazing.

The common PVC frames and wooden frames can actually perform 40% better than standard metal frames. Using "low-E" coating on the inner pane of double glazing can improve up to a 30% the performance of windows. Argon gas between the double glazings, improves the overall performance of windows more.

The following table demonstrates the influence of frames, glazing panes and spacers. According to the values, following points are obvious:
- A single glazing's values despite of frame material is quite low.
- For simple double glazing, the influence of frame is considerable and will make the value double.
- Using argon will considerably increase the value.
- There is no big difference between triple glazing filled with argon and quadruple glazing filled with krypton.

Insulation of windows is quite necessary and rewarding, while as an example, the heat loss in a medium glazed house (where glazing area is around 10% of total external surface) with standard double glazing windows is around 25–30%, the energy loss through the roof which is 30% of total external surfaces is only around 10% of the heat losses (Donn Michael, Grant Thomas, 2010).

2.1.4 Reducing Heat Gains through Glazing
Coating glass or using tints can reduce solar heat gains without weakening visible light transmission property of the glass.

Based on coating or tints, new window glazing could be categorized as:
- Chemically or physically altered glass.
- Coated glass or tints.
- Multiple-layered assemblies.

2.2 Types of Glazing
The glazing types are subjected to various items. The most effective items related to windows glazing technologies.

2.2.1 Gas Fills
When multi glazing (windows with two, three or four panes) are used, it is recommended to fill the space between the glass panes with inert gases to improve the thermal performance of windows.

The inert gases (argon and krypton) have a higher resistance to heat flow than air and they are sealed between the window panes to decreased the window's U-factor (Özsen, Emma,. Lee, Tony,. 2010).

2.2.2 Heat Absorbing Tints
One of the most common and available solutions to reduce incoming solar radiation through windows is using heat absorb tints, which change the color of the glass. Tinted glass can absorb a big part of heat. It reduces solar heat gain coefficient, visible transmittance and glare. Tints are available in different colors.

While gray and bronze tinted windows almost equally reduce penetration of both light and heat, blue and green tinted windows allow greater penetration of visible light and reduce heat transfer, comparing with other colors. Black tinted glasses absorb light more than heat. A more advance technology is electro-chromic glass, an optical switching technology that its transmittance can vary. Based on the voltage applied to glass, the glass will change from clear to dark tinted in 3–5 minutes. By reversing the voltage, glass will be restored to clear. Windows equipped with electro-chromic glass can be used both for fenestration and solar control (Özsen, Emma,. Lee, Tony,. 2010).

2.2.3 Insulated (Double-Glazed, Triple-Glazed)
The insulated window refers to windows, which their glass panes have been spaced apart and sealed to create a single-glazed unit with an air

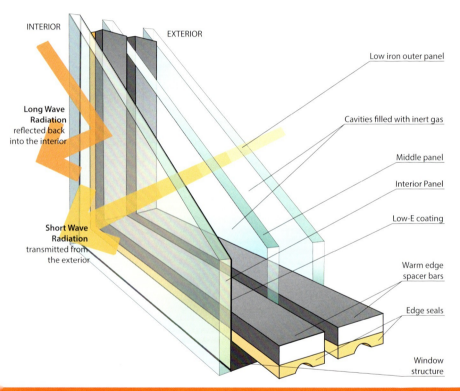

Fig. 12: Example of triple glazing

space between each pane of glass. The number of panes in each single unit could be two, three or more (see Fig. 12).

The glass layers and air spaces between them, together, will resist heat flow; therefore, insulated window glazing would lower the U-factor and consequently the solar heat gain coefficient too (Özsen, Emma,. Lee, Tony,. 2010).

2.2.4 Low-E (Low-Emissivity) Coatings

Low-E coating refers to microscopically thin glasses. They are made by depositing directly a layer of metal or metallic oxide on surface of panes of glass.

Even though Low-E glass is normally 10–15% more expensive than regular windows, they can reduce energy loss about 30–50% more, as they control heat transfer through the windows. The coated panes would allow short wave radiation of sun to enter the room, while long wave radiations (in form of heat) would be reflected back. The fact that made Low-E coating windows an optimal solution for an energy efficient construction.

The location of Low-E coating could be changed according to climate. While for hot climate, the Low-E coating should be applied to the outside pane of glass, for the cold climate, the coating should be applied to the inside panes of glass.

The Low-E coating glasses are lowering the U-factor of windows, by reducing the infrared radiation from warm panes of glass to the cooler panes. Low-E coating could be categorized based on allowance to solar gain as:

- High.
- Moderate.
- Low.

Low-E coating could also be categorized based on softness or hardness of coating as:

- Soft coating with a limited life span and better energy performance; would be easily damaged and degraded by being exposed to air and moisture.
- Hard coating with a longer life span and poorer energy performance; would be more durable and can be applied in retrofit applications (Özsen, Emma,. Lee, Tony,. 2010).

2.2.5 Spectrally Selective Coatings

Spectrally selective coatings filter out 40–70% of the heat normally transmitted through insulated window glass or glazing while allowing the full amount of light to be transmitted. Spectrally selective coatings are optically designed to reflect certain wavelengths but remain transparent to others. Such coatings are commonly used to reflect the infrared portion of the solar spectrum while admitting a higher portion of visible light. They help to create a window with a low U-factor and solar heat gain coefficient but a high visible transmittance. Spectrally selective coatings can be applied on various types of tinted glass to produce "customized" glazing systems capable of either increasing or decreasing solar gains according to desired aesthetic and climatic effects (Özsen, Emma,. Lee, Tony,. 2010).

2.2.6. Reflective Coatings
Reflective coating is referred to glass which consists of thin, metallic layers.[7] Applying reflective coating on window's glazing reduces the transmission of solar radiation and blocks light and heat[9]. Therefore, window's visible transmittance and glare will be reduced as well as window's solar heat gain coefficient (SHGC).

Even though reflective coating is appropriate for hot climates where heat gain control is a key issue; their application should be limited to the special cases. As using reflective coating besides reducing the heat gain will reduce the light transmittance as well, therefore, need for electric light would be increased. Reflective coating is applicable on single-pane glazing and double glazing where some coatings should be sealed inside the double-glass units (Özsen, Emma,. Lee, Tony,. 2010).

2.3 Thermal Performance of Different Glazing Types
U-factor of glazing and windows is an accurate indicator of thermal performance of glazing types (see Fig. 13).

2.3.1 Gas Fills
Proper combination of inert gases, using double or triple panes, frame with low-conductivity and Low-E coating can decrease U-factor down to 0.14.

Optimal space between panes is subjected to the used gas. While optimal spacing for argon is around 11–13 mm, for krypton, as a better option, is around 9 mm.

2.3.2 Heat Absorbing Tints
While applying heat absorbing tints cannot effectively reduce solar heat gain coefficient (SHGC), the reduction of visible transmittance is slightly larger.

Among the different color tints, green and blue are better options, as they allow more light in, while keeping heat out, black tinted glass are the worst, when the aim is reduction of cooling load, while black tinted glass absorb more visible energy than infrared energy.

2.3.3 Insulated (Double-Glazed, Triple-Glazed)
Double-glazed or triple-glazed are proper solutions to increase thermal performance of windows, as glass has higher heat conductivity in compare with air and gas. By trapping air between panes, it is possible to reduce the heat flow by half the amount of standard single glazing.

Using insulated double or triple glazing will move the thermal weak points to the edge of the unit, where glass is connected to frame.

Using thermal break (for metal frames), wooden or clad-wood sash frames or materials such as vinyl with lower thermal conductivity, will improve thermal performance of these weak points as well.

2.3.4 Low-Emissivity Coatings
One of the most effective options is using Low-E coating.

Through application of Low-E coating with insulated glazing, energy loss could decrease down to 50%. As mentioned before, soft coating is a better option, as the applied emissivity during manufacturing process of hard coating is between 0.15–2.0, for soft coating applied emissivity after manufacturing is between 0.05 and 0.10. They produce a lower U-value.

2.3.5 Spectrally Selective Coatings
A common indicator for performance of spectrally-selective glazing is the "light to solar" ratio (LSR). The LSR refers to ratio of visible light transmission divided by solar heat gain coefficient for a glazing system.

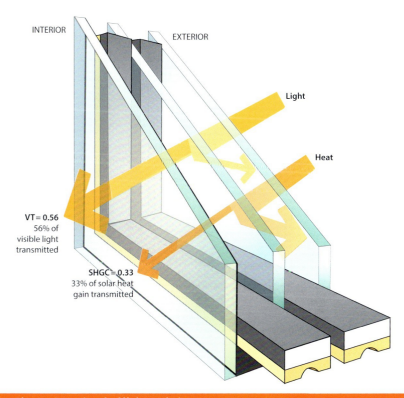

Fig. 13: Example of efficient window

The best possible ratio is close to 2.0. While a clear glazing unit has a value close to 1.0, a good spectrally-selective glazing could have normally a value greater than 1.7.

2.3.6 Reflective Coatings
As mentioned before, the most reflective glazing normally block daylight more than solar heat. Consequently, it is necessary to use additional elec-

tric lighting. Therefore, the possible reduction of heat gain would be compensating by the heat created by the additional electric lighting devices.

2.3.7 Emissive Value of Different Glazing Types
Representative emissivity values for different types of glass are as follows:
- Clear glass, uncoated: 0.84.
- Glass with single hard coat Low-E: 0.15.
- Glass with single soft coat Low-E: 0.10 (Özsen, Emma,. Lee, Tony,. 2010).

Glass Type (Product)	Visible Transmittance [% Daylight]	U-Factor	Solar Heat Gain Coefficient (SHGC)
Single Pane Glass (Standard clear)	89	1.09	0.81
Single White Laminated w/ Heat Rejecting Coating (South wall California Series®)	73	1.06	0.46
Double Pane Insulated Glass (Standard clear)	79	0.48	0.70
Double Bronze Reflective Glass (LOF Eclipse®)	21	0.48	0.35
Triple Pane Insulated Glass (Standard clear)	74	0.36	0.67
Pyrolitic Low-e Double Glass (LOF Clear Low-e®)	75	0.33	0.71
Soft-coat Low-e Double Glass w/Argon gas fill (PPG Sun gate® 100 Clear)	73	0.26	0.57
High Efficiency Low-e (Solar screen 2000 VEI-2M™)	70	0.29	0.37
Suspended Coated Film (Heat Mirror™ 66 Clear)	55	0.25	0.35
Suspended Coated Film w/ Argon gas fill (Azurlite® Heat Mirror SC75)	53	0.19	0.27
Double Suspended Coated Films w/Krypton (Heat Mirror™ 77 Super Glass)	55	0.10	0.34

Tab. 3: Comparison of glass types according visible transmittance, U-factor and solar heat gain coefficient (Passive Solar Design Guidelines)

2.4 Design Consideration
Windows and glazing, on every orientation, can provide useful daylight, but each orientation needs to be treated differently and Cons and Pros of each direction should be considered to maximize the expected benefits from glazing and windows.
- South: High quality consistent daylight with maximum heat gain in winter and minimal heat gain in summer. The thermal loss during

heating conditions should be considered in case of not using proper glazing types and window frames. Shading needed during hot days.
- North: Good access to strong illumination (the original source), even though very often varies throughout the day.
- East and West: Shading is difficult. Shading is critical for comfort and heat gain on both sides, especially on west. Windows facing north and south generally create fewest problems (O'Connor et al, 1997).

It is recommended, for excellent daylighting and glare control, to separate view and light windows.

Using clearer glazing with high-transmission, in high level (clerestory windows) and in lower view level in view windows lower-transmission glazing to control glare (O'Connor et al, 1997).

Diffuse glazing on the interior face and glass blocks redirects skylight to the deeper parts of the room, to a limited degree, from where the sky is not visible. The same type of prisms can also be used to redirect sunlight to the ceiling, giving shading in the front of the room, and generally increase daylight levels by diffuse reflection from the ceiling (Hastings, 1994).

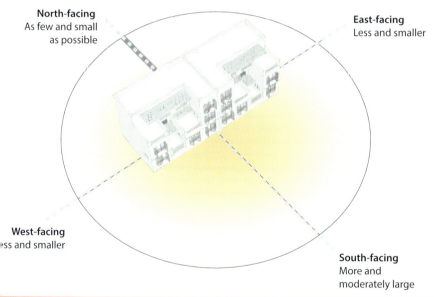

Fig. 14: Guidance for windows size in different direction

Insulated glazing units can be used to reduce the heat losses normally associated with single-glazed windows, allowing a good distribution of daylight (Hastings, 1994).

Glazing area should not be wasted where it cannot be seen, such as below desk height, as it wastes energy, causes discomfort (especially in winter) and provides little benefits.

Unobstructed south-facing glazing is best as:

- It captures solar energy in winter (when the sun is low in the sky).
- It is easier to shade from direct sun during summer (when the sun is high in the sky) by providing south-facing eaves, using plants and etc.

Where practical, the longest axis of a house should be oriented east-west to optimize the south-facing exposure. Rooms may also be stacked or staggered to achieve a greater south-facing aspect. Using south-facing clerestory windows and skylights provide possibilities to get direct sun deep into plan.

The practical depth of a daylight zone is typically limited to one-and-a-half times the window head height. With standard window and ceiling heights, adequate daylight extends to within 4.6 m from the window (O'Connor et al, 1997). Note that the higher the window is, the deeper the daylight reaches into the room.

The following principles should be considered when glazing is designed (O'Connor et al, 1997):

- Large windows require more measures to control glare and heat gains.
- Strip windows provide a uniform distribution of daylight.

Designing windows near the surface provides a better distribution. Because surfaces are facilitating more reflect and redistribute of daylight (Donn, Michael,. Grant, Thomas,. 2010).

3 Thermal Mass

Thermal mass is an old concept in designing a building which describes the effect of mass of the building (thermal storage capacity of building elements) in moderating internal temperature of the building and delaying the heat penetration from outside to inside of the building.

Iranian traditional architecture presents valuable examples of thermal mass, especially in hot areas in the edge of desert, where harsh climate could become moderate just by appropriate size and dimensions of walls and roofs. It shows how traditional architect used and took advantage of the thermal storage capacity of the building mass.

It works based on the fact that the mass can store heat and even out the temperature fluctuations in a hostile living environment. Proper consideration of this concept can increase the comfort level inside the building.

3.1. General Principles

Thermal mass can moderate internal temperatures by moderating day/night extremes (see Fig. 15).

Thermal mass could be more effective when is integrated with main passive design strategies such as:
- Orientation for easier shading.
- Appropriate areas of glazing.
- Appropriate levels of shading.
- Insulation (where effective).
- Night cooling.

3.1.1 How Thermal Mass Works

High thermal mass materials are able to reduce the need for heating and cooling. The obvious advantages of well-utilized thermal mass is the fact that energy from the sun is free.

Thermal mass is working in two ways as follows:
- *Absorbing direct solar radiation:* when the sun shines through windows onto a high thermal mass surface, the solar radiation is absorbed directly by the surface.[9]
- *Absorbing heat from air inside the building;* thermal mass absorbs heat from air inside a house when that air is hotter than the thermal mass.[10]

Due to density and higher mass, materials such as concrete floors and walls with higher thermal mass, need more energy and consequently more time. Therefore, process of heating up in high thermal mass materials is more slowly in compare with lightweight materials. The property that results in effective reduction of overheating and partial absorption of excess heat by thermal mass (see Fig. 15).

Whereas thermal mass must be insulated from direct contact with outside air and ground, for effective collecting the heat, thermal mass must not be isolated from inside of the house by any sort of insulating materials (Donn, Michael,. Grant, Thomas,. 2010).

3.1.2 Common Materials for Thermal Mass

In general, thermal mass could be provided through various ways; more common ways are as follows:
- Concrete blocks and other forms of concrete masonry.
- Concrete floor slabs.
- Precast concrete.
- Ceramic and concrete-tiles.
- Water: water has the highest volumetric heat capacity of all commonly used materials.
- Insulated concrete panels consist of an inner layer of concrete to provide the thermal mass factor.

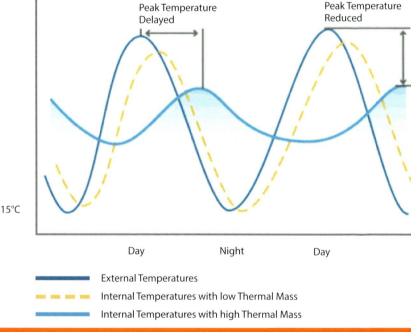

Fig. 15: How thermal mass can moderate temperature fluctuations (Design Comfortable Home)

- Insulating concrete forms are commonly used to provide thermal mass in building structures.
- Clay bricks, adobe bricks or mud-bricks.
- Earth, mud and lawn (Grass or sod).
- Rammed earth (compacting soil between temporary formwork to build a solid block of earth).
- Natural rock and stone.

V | Applicable Measures for Building Physic

- Logs (trunk of trees) are used as a building material to create the exterior and perhaps also the interior walls of homes.

3.1.3 Proper Amount and Dimension of Thermal Mass

The effectiveness of thermal mass is depended on various factors such as: thickness of insulation, position of insulation, position of glass, dimension and area of glass, climate, and geographical properties of site and location of building in the site. The more involving factors, the more complicated the interaction between them. Therefore, it is not easy to generalize and suggest an exact amount regarding thermal mass, in fact, like insulation the more is not always the best. There are some basic principles that should be considered such as:

- In south facing spaces, large area of thermal mass should be in contact with the air that gets significant sun. The surface could be consisted of floor, walls and etc.

There is an optimal thickness for storage of heat from day to night, because thermal mass in some points absorb the heat and in other time the heat flow is reverse.

As an example the optimal thickness for concrete is between 100–200 mm and beyond this has no added benefit in terms of solar energy storage by thermal mass (Özsen, Emma,. Lee, Tony,. 2010).

3.1.4 Thermal Mass and Energy Efficiency

A building with high thermal mass could be energy efficient when it is properly insulated and has proper glazing. In fact, without insulation it is too difficult to heat a high mass building, as normally thermal mass is a good heat conductor. So there is no point in collecting the solar heat in a wall without a proper insulation. The same way there is no point to think without a proper and well-designed glazing, just by having sun shine on surface of the wall, it is possible to properly collect the solar heat energy.

Energy efficiency through thermal mass requires a design where solar heat is appropriately brought inside and heats the proper insulated thermal mass inside the space (Donn, Michael,. Grant, Thomas,. 2010).

3.2 Combined Types of Thermal Mass
3.2.1 Mass Storage Systems

In a mass storage system the collection, storage and transport of solar energy is combined in one unit. Therefore, it simultaneously allows the building to function as a solar collector and storage device. Trombe wall is a good example of a combined unit. It works on a basic greenhouse principle. A trombe wall is particularly suited for buildings that have significant heat load during night. The release of heat from mass during night can avoid or minimize the need for auxiliary heating (Hastings, 1994).

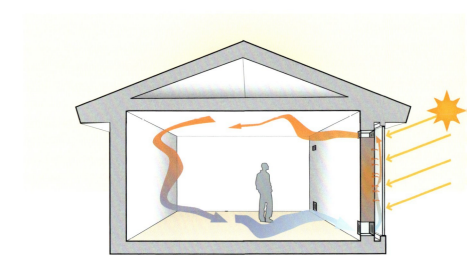

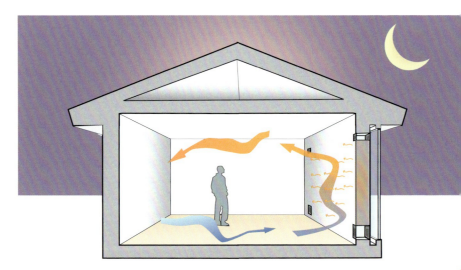

Fig. 16: A trombe wall

3.2.2 Thermal Mass & Transparent Insulation Systems

The performance of a standard thermal mass wall system can be greatly improved with transparent insulation as glazing. Solar radiation is partially transmitted through the insulation to be absorbed at the exterior surface of the wall. Depending on solar radiation, the wall heats up and temporarily transfers heat from outside to inside (see Fig. 16). During periods of weak or no radiation, heat losses are minimized by the insulation level of the material layer on the outside of the wall. In periods of higher radiation, external walls absorb radiation; store heat and can temporarily heat the surface of adjoining space (Hastings, 1994).

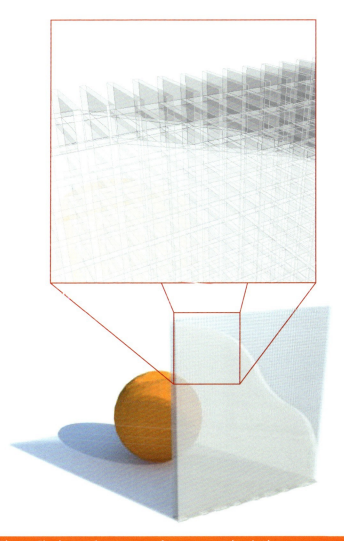

Fig. 17: The internal structure of transparent insulation

3.2.3 Thermal Labyrinths

Thermal mass can be used within an air delivery system to moderate the temperature of supply air. This system includes simple solutions such as running air supply "ducts" inside hollow concrete structure.

Unlike thermal mass used in building envelope that is designed to control heat variations over a day, a thermal labyrinth is designed to moderate over an entire year. Surplus heat is removed from air coming into the building during summer and is retained until the winter, when it is used to warm the cooler incoming air. Therefore this system require quite large amounts of mass to maintain a stable temperature over a full year. This, along with the space requirements, make thermal labyrinths a bit expensive (see Fig. 17). As mentioned before, a simpler and cheaper solution is to use concrete structure of the building as an air-delivery system, ducting the air through hollow concrete beams, or within hollow-core or sine-wave slabs. Another similar system is "ground source heating". In this case pipes are laid horizontally below the surface and used to draw air along them and into the building (Ministry for the Environment of New Zealand, 2008).

3.3 Typical Thermal Mass Applications

In cold temperature climates, thermal mass is often used as heat storage to absorb solar heat gain which is used to heat the interior of buildings. In Tehran however, thermal mass should be used to aid in both passive cooling and heating.

As mentioned in the above sections, thermal mass can moderate internal temperatures by averaging the day/night extremes, and by creating a delay in the occurrence of peak internal temperature as compared to the external temperature.

In order to be used for passive cooling and heating, both following issues should be considered (see Fig. 19).

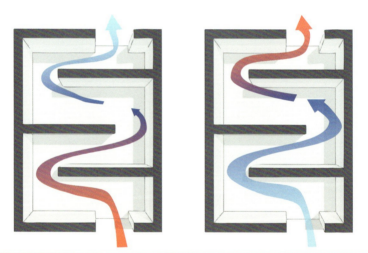

Fig. 18: A thermal labyrinth and a rockbin

Solar exposed thermal mass
Thermal mass is placed within the building and situated where it still can be exposed to low angle winter sunlight (via windows) but insulated from heat loss. In summer thermal mass should be obscured from higher angle summer sunlight in order to prevent over-heating of the structure.

Thermal mass for limiting summertime over-heating
Thermal mass is placed within a building where it is protected from direct solar gain but exposed to the building occupants.

The most common ways in naturally ventilated or low energy mechanically ventilated buildings are:
- Solid concrete floor slabs.
- Concrete roof (soffit) exposed to occupied space.
- Thermal mass as heat storage in form of both concrete exterior and interior walls.
- Thermal mass as heat storage in form of intermediate floors and staircases.

It should be mentioned that many homeowners prefer to have carpets or similar floor coverings which can isolate the thermal mass and thereby reduce its heat storage effect. Therefore, relying on thermal mass of a floor slab alone may be unwise, as it is possible that the floor to be carpeted at some stage (Özsen, Emma,. Lee, Tony,. 2010).

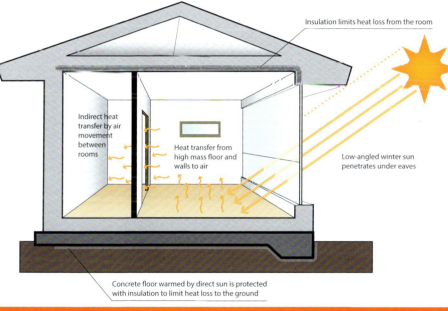

Fig. 19: Thermal mass application

3.3.1 Thermal Properties of Common Materials
High density
The denser the materials (i.e. the higher mass per unit volume), the higher is their thermal mass. As an example, standard concrete has a high thermal mass but aerated concrete blocks have a lower thermal mass.

Good thermal conductivity
The material must allow heat to flow through it. As an example whereas reinforced concrete is a good conductor, rubber is a poor conductor of heat.[11]

Low reflectivity
Low reflectivity is another necessary property, as the more matt and rough the surface is, the more energy will be absorbed and re-radiate (Özsen, Emma,. Lee, Tony,. 2010).[12]

3.4 Design Consideration
There are many thermal mass systems commonly used. Thermal mass could be sorted out as heating or cooling. In order to have thermal mass functioning properly, the difference between systems should be noticed and considered.

Passive heating: Thermal mass with direct heat gain (L)
In the best form, thermal mass should be directly exposed to the sun throughout the day. It is recommended that the ratio between mass and glass area to be minimum 3:1. Recommendation of higher ratios of up to 9:1 depends on mass type, exposure, thickness, occupancy patterns, energy requirements and climate of area (Rinaldi, Nicola, 2009).

Passive heating: Thermal mass with indirect heat gain
Different indirect gain systems commonly in use are: trombe walls, water walls, roof ponds and sun spaces. In indirect heat gain systems, thermal mass separates the collector from conditioning space.
- Trombe wall: Commonly constructed of concrete or masonry, trombe wall should be placed directly between south-facing aperture and the interior space. The use of night insulation will considerably increase the efficiency of the system.
- The water wall: It should be placed between south-facing aperture and the space, as it will increase overall heat capacity. Air circulation between the collector and the space is not limited by loosely placed water containers. Night insulation could improve the efficiency of the system.
- The roof pond: In this case thermal mass is placed in the roof structure. It depends on a switchable, exterior insulation scheme to make the system effective for both heating and cooling conditions. While the insulation in heating mode is deployed at nights, in the cooling mode insulation is deployed during daytimes. The thermal mass, water in containers such as waterbed mattresses, must be in direct thermal contact with the interior of the building, normally a structural steel deck is the optimal thermal connector for this purpose (Rinaldi, Nicola, 2009 & Haglund, Bruce,. Rathmann, Kurt, 1996).

Passive cooling: High-mass
A high-mass cooling system uses mass to store internal heat gains which are flushed each night by using natural ventilation or fans.

A hybrid solution of mechanical forced-air handler integrated with high-mass cooling can effectively function. The walls and floors should be flushed with night air both at their surfaces and through the floor's hollow cores (Haglund,Bruce,. Rathmann, Kurt, 1996).

Passive cooling: Courtyards
In this effective system, a thermally massive courtyards floor surrounded by a building buffered with a shade-giving arcade can provide cooling, through radiation to the cool and clear night sky. Night time radiation cools the mass and the air trapped in the courtyard. The cool air is drawn into the building, replacing warmer air which rises. Provided arcade can protect the building from direct solar gain during daytimes. The cool mass in the courtyard floor can absorb big parts of the solar radiation.

It is recommended, in order to have the most thermally effective courtyards, the mass floor to have an unobstructed view of the night sky, in other words no trees or vegetation should block the radiant path.

Active heating: Water ponds
The essential ingredients of an effective active heating system are rock beds and water storage tanks. In this system mass is used to store thermal energy to be used for heating on demand. When appropriate size of thermal mass is used, it would be possible to manage thermal energy both diurnally and seasonally. In an active system, thermal mass should be thermally isolated from both the collector and the conditioned space. Therefore, it is possible to store heat all summer for winter use (Haglund,Bruce,. Rathmann, Kurt, 1996).

Active heating: Phase change materials (PCMs)
This system takes advantage of the energy stored and released during change-of-state, materials that have a melting point near room temperature.

Therefore, it is provides thermal mass without bulk of large masonry structures or large water containers. Even though the potential for PCMs is quite great, the technical problems with storage and endurance has limited widespread use of this system (Rinaldi, Nicola, 2009 & Haglund,

Bruce,. Rathmann, Kurt, 1996).

4 Daylighting

Daylighting is an effective way to use windows and skylights to allow the sunlight enter the building. The appropriate applying of daylighting concept could reduce the needs of artificial lighting systems.

After introducing energy efficient advanced windows and advanced and modern lighting design systems, efficient use of windows and daylighting during the daylight hours, without serious conflict with heating and cooling issues, is easier.

There are different factors influencing daylighting, such as: geographical conditions, climate, urban form, urban regulations and codes, building codes, building design, size and location of windows and etc.

South-facing windows are the most beneficial ones for providing daylighting and controlling the heat gain and loss through the windows.

South-facing windows in north spare of earth, allow most winter sunlight into the building and less direct sun during the summer when properly shaded.

Even though it is possible to have a good daylight penetration in morning and evening from the east- and west-facing windows; due to the glare and considerable heat gain in summer and little heat gain in winter, they should be limited to the minimum size or avoided completely (Ministry for the Environment of New Zealand, 2008).

Benefits of daylighting
Using daylighting can lead to improvements in life-cycle cost of the buildings, increase user productivity in work spaces, reduce CO_2 emissions, operating costs and overall energy consumption of buildings (Özsen, Emma,. Lee, Tony,. 2010).

4.1 General Principles
An awareness of basic visual perception and issues related to higher performance is necessary for an effective daylighting design.
- *Veiling reflections:* Veiling reflections of high brightness light sources by reducing contract. It is very important to control and avoid such an effect where critical visual tasks are carried out.
- *Distribution:* Introducing appropriate daylight as much as deep as possible into a building interior. As human eye can adjust to high levels of luminance as long as it is evenly distributed; it is recommended to introduce light as much as possible when is indirect and evenly distributed.[13]
- *Glare:* Glare or excessive brightness contrast within the field of view is a discomforting effect of light for occupants and one of the aspects of lighting. A human eye cannot function properly when an extreme level of brightness is presented in the field of view.

- Variety: Variety in brightness light is a desirable quality; while uniform light can lead to tiredness. Therefore, a good design brings some sort of contrast in brightness for some visual effectiveness. In a good solution for daylighting, a blast of beam day-light is integrated in a circulation area to guide occupants through the building.[14]

Appropriate design pays special attention to the qualitative and quantitative aspects of daylighting.

It is recommended to provide an adequate light level according to function and activities in the space. It could be a proper combination of natural and artificial sources. On the other hand, for effective lighting, the daylighting should be integrated with electric lighting systems. Increasing the overall efficiency of the lighting system and net-energy saving, asks for coupling daylighting with an efficient electric lighting control. This could be presented through an application of continuously dimming fixtures controlled by luminous sensors.

Light transmission
Light transmission refers to the fact that even though the transparent object is transmitting the light, not all the light passes through. As an example, a window with thick glass or tinted glass will not allow all the light pass through. Here, part of the light will be absorbed by the medium through which it passes. Therefore, the transmitted beam has lower intensity of the incident beam. The Ratio of the intensities depends on the intensity of incident beam and transmitted beam.

Compromise between daylighting and heat gain control
There is a direct relation between daylighting and heat gaining. In the area with hot climate, it is especially important to consider this fact and look for solutions, which can control the overall heat gain through daylighting. There are various solutions such as:
- Spectrally selective coating, where coating can block most of infrared and ultraviolet radiations, while allowing visible light spectrum through the glass.
- Tubular skylight which is consisted of roof mounted light or solar collectors is another solution which increases the daylighting potentials. As the rooftop solar collector has small surface area, tubular skylights minimize heat gain in summer as well as heat loss in winter (Özsen, Emma,. Lee, Tony,. 2010).

4.2 Design Consideration
Daylighting design is in fact the consideration of the interactions among light quality, climate conditions, building function, orientation, occupant's behaviors, solar gain and building design.

4.2.1 Building Form

Selecting an appropriate building footprint can allow a building to maximize the use of available daylight, where long narrow footprints are preferable to square ones (O'Connor et al, 1997). The following floor plans are some examples of layouts that effectively distribute and use daylight (see Fig. 20). Buildings with long and narrow sections allow daylight into the floor plate at most.

The following features should also be included where possible (O'Connor et al, 1997) (see Fig. 21):

- North-South windows (within 15 degrees of the South-North axis in both directions is acceptable).
- Windows on two sides of rooms, for better daylight distribution.
- The depth of room should be within 1.5 to 2 times of window head height, for a better light level and distribution.

4.2.2 Layout and Location of Spaces

Layout of rooms and different spaces should be designed according to the functions and tasks of space and required light for better performance of those tasks.

Tasks requiring higher light levels with regular performances should be located near windows, and tasks with little need for daylight with infrequently and less performances can be located in distant from windows.

Fig. 20: Building footprints for best daylight access

Furniture layout should not block incoming light into spaces further from the window (O'Connor et al, 1997). If partitions are necessary, using translucent materials in upper parts of partitions could be a solution (O'Connor et al, 1997).

Selecting appropriate materials for surfaces is another important consideration.

Surface materials with high reflectance are better choices as they re-

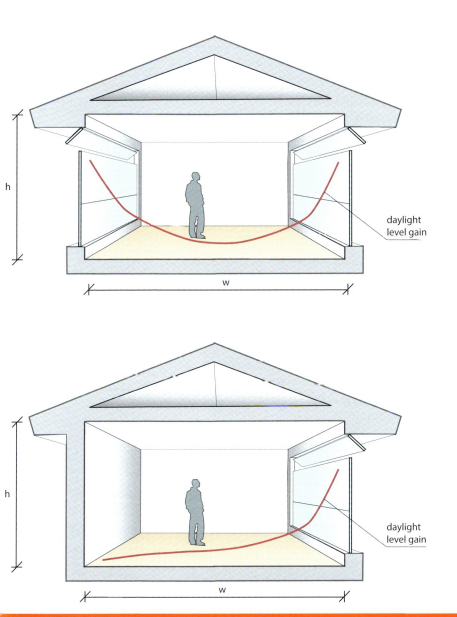

Fig. 21: Daylighting guidelines for room dimensions

sult higher light levels at rear part of space a more even light distribution.

For emphasizing on keeping distance from windows, dark surfaces could be possible choices (O'Connor et al, 1997).

The recommended surface reflectance is:
- Ceilings: > per cent.
- Walls: 50–70 per cent.
- Floors: 20–45 per cent.

Using a sloped ceiling is another way of improving daylight distributions at rear part of a space and increasing depth while proper level of light is still provided. Locating ducting at the back of the space will also allow high windows to fit within the standard floor-to-ceiling height (see Fig. 22) (Hastings, 1994) (Ministry for the Environment of New Zealand, 2008).

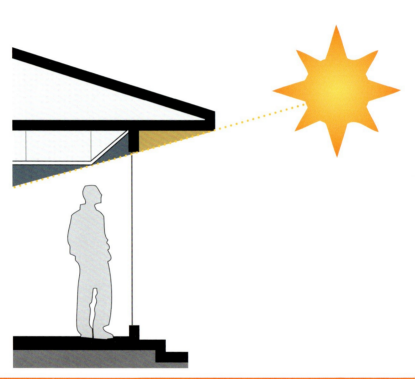

Fig. 22 : The use of a sloped celling to improve daylight penetration into a room

5 Shading and Avoiding Overheating

In most parts of Iran generally and in Tehran in particular, there is a high potential of overheating in hot months. There are different solutions to avoid unwanted solar gain as well as getting rid of excess heat resulted from overheating.

Even though through appropriate thermal mass and insulation it is possible to control overheating, it is not always sufficient. There are few passive effective ways to control and avoid overheating such as:
- *Shading:* Appropriate shading can block the sun when it is not wanted.
- *Cross-ventilate:* Providing possibility of cross-ventilation in house could help to get rid of excess heat.

The active common ways of avoiding overheating are as follows:
- Air conditioners.
- Tinted windows (or coated with reflective film).

Fig. 23: The effect of shading to limitate sunlight penetration into a room

Provide shading
A simple way to avoid overheating from the sun is to provide appropriate overhangs above south-facing windows and external shading on east- and west-facing windows.

An appropriate overhang projecting above a window works well on south of a house while it controls the radiation of the sun inside the space, when it is high in the sky in summer and heat is undesirable. In winter and cold moths, an appropriate overhang let the sun shine in through the windows, when heat is most wanted. It should be mentioned that overhangs are ineffective against the low-angled morning sun from east and the late afternoon sun from west. In such situations a vertical screen, such as an external louvers shutter or a blind is more effective. Furthermore, using movable louvers can allow access to view when the sun is not considered as a trouble (see Fig. 23).

Sun shades are available in the form of awnings or other similar devices. As heat will be trapped under and behind the dark colored shading devices, it is recommended to use sun-shading devices with light color (see Fig. 24).

Appropriate shadings can be very effective, as they can reduce summer temperature by blocking up to 90 percent of direct sunlight. This effect can considerably improve comfort and save energy (Donn, Michael,. Grant, Thomas,. 2010).

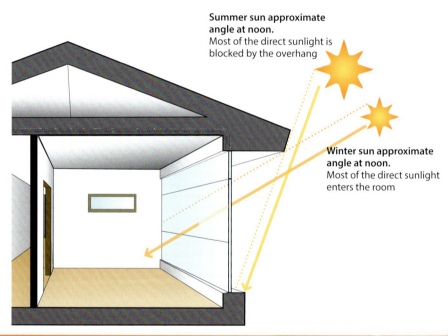

Fig. 24 : Effectiveness and function of overhang in summer and winter

5.1 General Principles

As it has been already mentioned, radiating heat from the sun can (mostly are partially depended on glazing types) pass through glass into the space behind. Building elements (windows, frames, walls and etc.) as well as potential furniture inside the spaces, after absorbing the heat will re-radiate this heat again but with different wavelength. Therefore, the absorbed heat cannot be radiate out through the glass to the outside space.

In this context, it is very important to use proper shading for windows, which avoids radiant heat get trapped inside the space. Furthermore, shaded glass is somehow protected against the glare by blocking direct sunlight penetration. In fact, appropriate shading allows diffuse daylight pass through the glass (see Fig. 25).

In case of area with high altitude, it is important to provide shading for walls and roof surfaces, as well.

There is a strong relationship between shading and orientation, whereas the main shading considerations might be defined according to the orientation of the building. For example, elongation of the building to east-west axis, will affect shading design of the building and is more at-

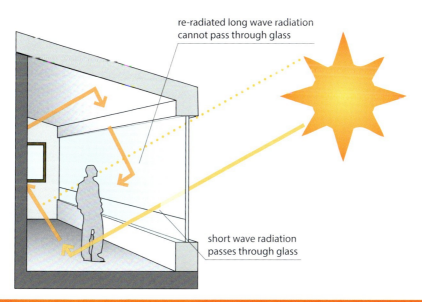

Fig. 25: Example of heat transmission through windows

tainable. Whereas south-facing windows and walls can be easily shaded from direct sunlight by using simple overhangs (eaves) or louvers, east-west windows or elongation of the building in this direction, makes shading more difficult and complicated, as it is too difficult to control "low angle" lights from east and west. It requires vertical shading which in turn can obstruct the view and reduce the possibility of daylight from these directions.

Fig. 26: Example of simple shading

It is recommended to use wide overhangs, in the mid-morning and early afternoon, when the sun angle is not very low. However they can only be useful in the early afternoon and mid-morning when the sun angle is not very low. The most common and simple shading art illustrated in Figure 26.

Some simple and consequently cost effective methods which can be used for shading east and west facing sides of a house are presented in

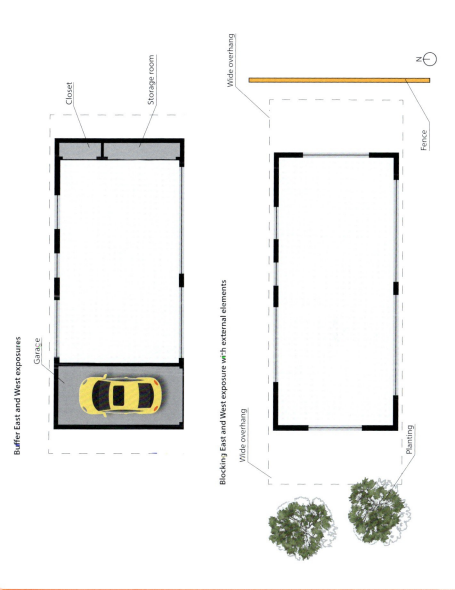

Fig. 27: Example of cost effective shading strategies for east or west sides

Figure 27. Using trees or vegetated fences can facilitate blocking of low angle sun rays allowing diffuse daylight pass through the windows. East and west facing areas without air-conditioned spaces behind could work as buffering or insulating spaces (Özsen, Emma,. Lee, Tony,. 2010).

5.2 Types of Shading

Fixed shading

These types of shading are good choices for south sides of building. Whereas adequate controlling or even blocking the radiation of summer sun is quite important, allowing the winter sun to pass through is also very essential. Therefore, it requires precise calculation of width, depth and location of shading (see Fig. 28).

Movable shading

Using movable shading gives some degree of freedom to the occupants to adjust the shading according to need.

It is recommended to use them especially for east and west sides, as it is too difficult to provide sufficient protection against low angle sun lights through fixed shading devices.

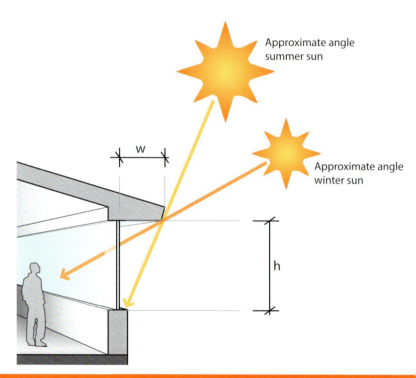

Fig. 28: Allowing sun penetration in winter

There are more advanced devices, which provide more choices such as: allowing all sun in, excluding all sun or letting in certain angle and level of sun. It is recommended to use these devices for south-east or south-west windows, which are exposed to combination of low and high angle sun during the day. Louvers, shutters, retractable awnings, sliding screens and adjustable blinds are some common examples of movable and adjustable shading devices.

Shading using plants
One of the oldest methods of providing shadings is using plants. Plants are not only providing natural shading, but also they can provide some sort of privacy and filtering air and noise.

It is important to choose proper trees for shading. As an example, not every green tree is a good option when letting the sun light and heat pass through the spaces is desired; as another example trees with high canopies are good options when shading of roof or bigger part of building is required.

Shrubs are more adequate choices for lower windows. Wall vines and other sort of plants which are growing on the surface of walls, are useful against summer heat, they can also reduce reflection radiations. Ground covers have indirect effect, as they are absorbing the sun heat without re-radiating it to the building (see Fig. 30) (Özsen, Emma,. Lee, Tony,. 2010).

Roller shutter blinds   Adjustable awning

Fig. 29: Examples of movable shading (adjustable awning and roller shutter blinds)

Fig. 30: Examples of using trees as shading devices

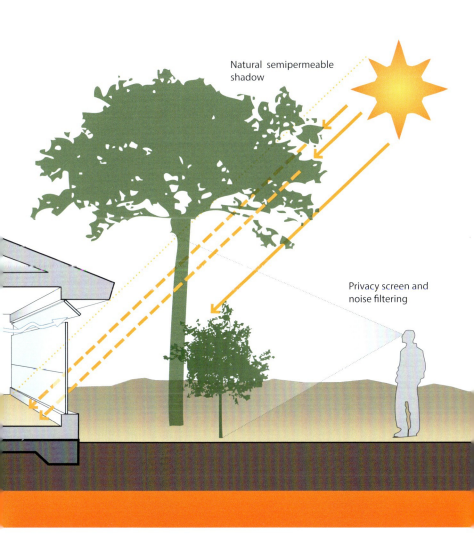

5.3 Shading and Daylight

There is sort of a conflict between shading and day-lighting. Therefore, it is important to be careful about selected measures for shading in order not to reduce considerable benefits of daylighting.

When designing shading and day-lighting, it is also important to distinguish between daylight and sunlight. While daylighting refers to level of diffuse natural light which can come inside the space from the surrounding sky dome or reflected off adjacent surfaces, sunlight refers to direct sunshine which is brighter than ambient daylight.

The other important differences are: glare which can disturb work surfaces or be reflected off a computer screen and heat gain which in case of sunlight could cause excessive heat gain.

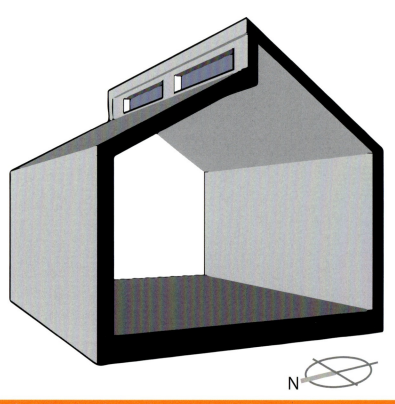

Fig. 31: Examples of use of clerestories for daylight

There are different solutions to benefit from daylight while avoiding direct sunlight, such as:

- Using certain types of plants which allow filtered light pass into the building while providing shading.
- Using "clerestories" which are not exposed to direct sunlight (see Fig. 31).
- Using light color external surfaces or shading devices, which can reflect light into the building.
- Using light shelves which can function as shading devices and light reflectors (Özsen, Emma,. Lee, Tony,. 2010).

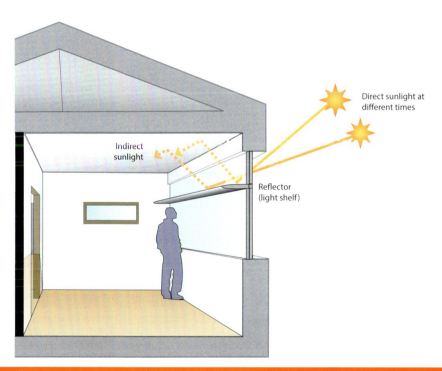

Fig. 32: Examples of use of light shelf as a reflector

5.4 Design Consideration

There are lots of similarities between shading design considerations and day-lighting design considerations, as an optimal shading solution should be correspondent (compatible) with day-lighting considerations as well as other strategies adopted in the building construction process. There are several possible design options.

Overhangs and sidefins

As the main consideration regarding permanent overhangs and sidefins (overhangs for high angle summer sun and sidefins for low angle sun in winter, morning and afternoon) it is necessary to design their dimensions according to the sun angle and orientation of the windows.

The overhangs are optimal choices for south facing windows. For east and west, sidefins are better options.

It should be mentioned that using permanent device like overhangs has several advantages such as: having less effect on view, allowing low-angle winter sun to come inside the space and blocking high-angle summer sunshine (see Fig. 33).

Fixed louvres

Louvers should be carefully selected to be efficient in controlling undesirable sunlight.

The important parameters are depth of blades, space between blades and orientation of blades. The same as overhangs, while the horizontal

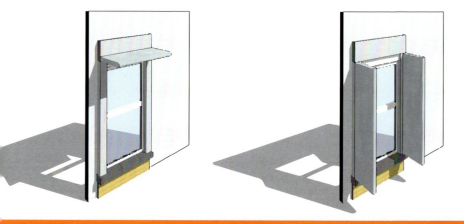

Fig. 33: Overhangs (left) and sidefins (right)

louvres are the best options for southern windows, where the main issue is controlling high angle sun radiation, the best option for west and east windows is vertical louvres. The other possible options for west and east windows are external blades or mesh screen. For maximum efficiency louvres could be automated.

The two important issues to be considered in selecting and designing the louvres are: maintenance of louvres and influence of louvres on view.

It should be noticed that horizontal and vertical louvres have basic differences, where as horizontal louvres are the best at blocking high angle sun light, vertical louvres are the best to block low angle morning and afternoon sun light. Normally they placed in front of windows in exterior space (see Fig. 34).

Light shelves
Light shelves block direct sun while reflecting daylight off the room's ceiling, deep into the space.

Roller blinds and internal louvers
Roller blinds and internal louvers are another adjustable shading devices.
They allow occupants to adjust the blinds and louvers according the source of glare, therefore, they are considered as a good option for effective glare control.

As a main advantage, they can be easily retrofitted into wide variety of buildings, therefore, they can be considered as recyclable materials.

There are few disadvantages associated with internal movable louvers such as: obscuring the external view, trapping absorbed solar gain between louvers and windows and releasing them into the interior space. The later disadvantages could be decreased through using reflective materials, but this solution can cause glare, which is also undesirable.

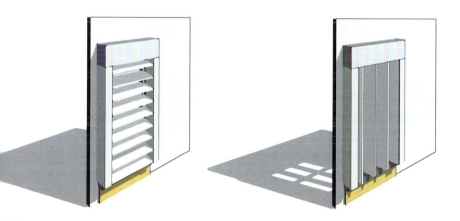

Fig. 34: Horizontal and vertical louvres

Screens
The size and dimension of mesh screens are a bite different with other shading devices. They can be hanged around the building and provide a remarkable aesthetic feature (see Fig. 35). Due to the structure of mesh screen, there are several advantages such as:
·· Providing an especial event around the building, which is very different with "all or nothing" effect of louvers.

- Providing occupants with a reasonable visual connection to the external view through their evenness.
- Providing different levels of transparency according to size of the mesh.
- Providing possibility of green façades through combination of climbing plant with metal grids.
- Providing aesthetic features and decreasing visual impact of the building by providing green façades on its sides.

As disadvantages, following could be mentioned:
- Screen mesh could be quite expensive.
- Green screens need high maintenance and need regular irrigation.

Double skin façades

Double skin façade is referring to the sheltered space in front of convention space. It could be separated from outside space by blinds, louvers,

Fig. 35: A green-screen with the two meshes hung on the solid façade
Note: The image shows a mature green-screen in use. Note that for shading purposes the green-screen should extend over the windows.

glass, and screen mesh or by another transparent façade. Double skin façade can provide the occupants with movable shading which blocks undesirable sunlight passes through the space. The double skin facade could function manually or automatically. It could be controlled through light sensors on the façade which can raise, lower and open or close the blinds. Therefore, it could provide comfortable conditions throughout days and nights (see Fig. 36).

As already mentioned, light shelves and clerestories can be used to allow daylight into the room (in this case with s sloped perimeter ceiling). they can be integrated with the double skin façade's maintenance walkways, which can also act as a diffuse overhang.

As the best location, a double skin façade should be placed in south facing side, where it could receive as much as possible heat from the sun to assist natural heating and natural ventilation for the building.

Due to the necessities of having double glazing, double skin façades can be expensive.

Double façade could be integrated with other passive design strategies, such as light shelves or natural ventilation.

The other form of double skin façades could include a terrace that could be extension of room behind the façade according to the needs and desires of occupants (Ministry for the Environment of New Zealand, 2008).

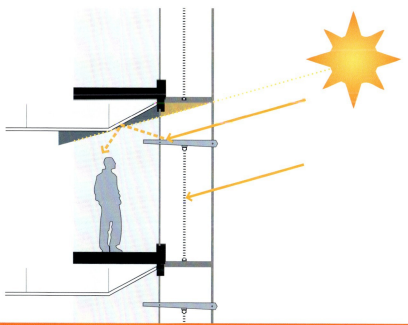

Fig. 36: Shading strategies within a double skin façade, with blinds hung between the two glazing skins.

143

6 Ventilation

Ventilation in general, refers to all activities associated with providing desirable air inside the building such as: removing excessive solar heat, facilitating air movement, bringing fresh air inside while sending the polluted and unpleasant air outside through windows, doors and sometimes unglazed vents.

Winter case
winter winds are moslty dissipated by dense evergreen planting

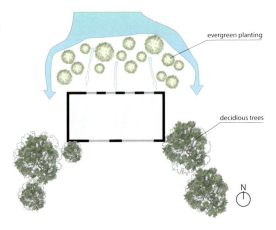

Summer case
summer breezes are directed towards buiding through decidious trees

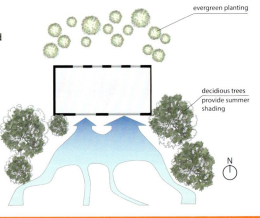

Fig. 37: Applicable measures

Appropriate ventilation requires careful design and layout for inside and outside (placing open spaces and elements around the building).

As an example, the trees, hedges and windbreakers which are meant to provide shelters for cold months, might be designed in a way that allow and facilitate the cooling summer breezes to penetrate inside the buildings. Therefore, considering appropriate location and size of windows, doors and trees are the key elements in ventilation (see Fig. 37).

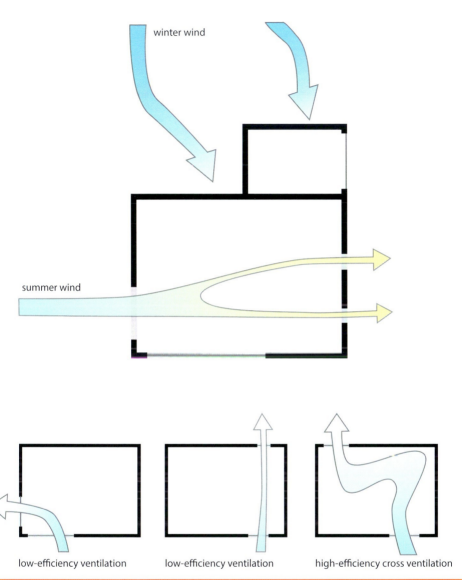

Fig. 38: Different location of opening for natural ventilation

There are several key factors which are considered as basis for a good venting system such as:
- Positioning the opening and windows on opposite walls.
- Positioning openings and windows at different heights.
- Positioning openings and windows not directly in the same line across a space.

- Openings and windows should be large enough to allow fresh and good air flow inside.
- Openings and windows should be able to be shut completely and seal well against cold winter air.
- Openings and windows should be able to be locked in a partially open position to allow continues cooling while still secured.
- Openings and windows should be able to provide enough protection, especially for children not to fall out of them.

These will ensure cooling breezes to pass through the entire building and occupied space to provide cooling for those who are inside the space (see Fig. 38).

Using mechanical devices such as well-designed, low-energy ceiling fans can provide air movement and therefore pleasant cooling during hot days.

In combination with other passive measures considered in process of design and construction of buildings, this could provide quite sufficient cooling during hot months.

The natural effect of warm air rising up could be increased by incorporating a natural chimney through the building. The optimal location for this opening is the rooftop. They might be enough large to facilitate the air flow. Ventilation devices should be fully adjustable to control airflow on cold days (see Fig. 39) (Donn, Michael,. Grant, Thomas,. 2010).

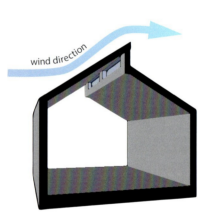 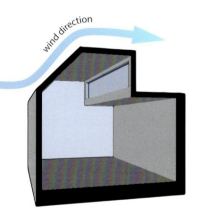

Fig. 39: Matching opening type to roof pitch

6.1 General Principles

As mentioned before, appropriate ventilation and providing optimal possibility for air movement are important items in energy efficiency of buildings. Ventilation can be categorized in two main groups as natural and mechanical ventilation; however using combination of both groups is quite common. There are two main natural effects which can drive natural ventilation:

- Natural ventilation driven by the climate forces of wind (wind effect ventilation).
- Natural ventilation driven by temperature differences (stack effect ventilation) (see Fig. 40).

Mechanical ventilation is functioning more based on air movements. Creating air movement in building will lead to better cooling effects through increasing evaporation. There is a physiological cooling effect associated with air movement; movement of still air at a certain speed, will cause occupants feel less hot.

In spite of natural or mechanical ventilation, air movement and air exchange are key factors.

For instance, while cross ventilation (as the most effective means of natural ventilation for cooling the buildings) is functioning through air

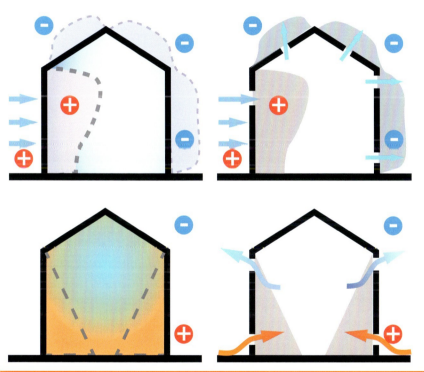

Fig. 40: Wind effect (pressure driven) ventilation (left), stack effect (temperature driven) ventilation (right)

exchange, a fan (as an effective means of mechanical cooling) is useful for enhancing air movement for cooling the building occupants.

Direct ventilation
There are places in buildings which are producing heat and water vapor such as kitchens or bathrooms. This condition requires direct ventilation. Even though the amount of produced heat cannot be a serious problem,

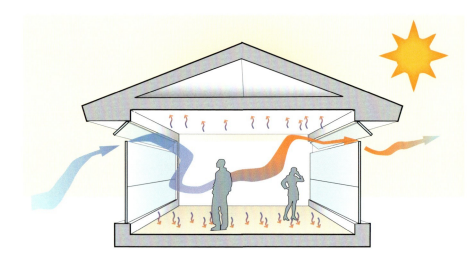

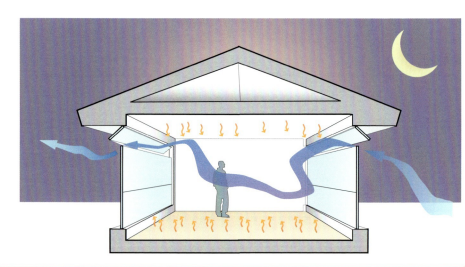

Fig. 41: Stack ventilation examples

the water vapor, if allowed to be condensed, can cause serious health difficulties as well as unpleasant scenes and problems regarding overall maintenance of building.

Therefore, it is important to prevent condensation and extracting the water vapor outside the building.

Normally extractor fans with relatively high ventilation rates are used to extract the waste air directly to the outside.

Heat distribution
Another means of energy efficiency in buildings could be the proper distribution of heat from warmer areas to the areas where received a little direct sunlight. This can be easily achieved through combination of: taking advantages of natural effect of warm air rising and mechanical ventilation system.[15]

A fan with a thermostat control could be an optimal low-cost solution. The function of thermostat is to ensure that the system functions according to certain designs and programs, even when occupants are not there or not taking notice.

The control over the openings of system is also important, as it will allow keeping control where and when the heat should be distributed. As this system needs movement of huge amounts of air to effectively function, the size of openings is an important issue (Donn, Michael,. Grant, Thomas,. 2010).

Night cooling
Thermal mass is designed to absorb heat gain during days and that reduces the peak temperature. The absorbed heat by the thermal mass should be taken out of the building so that it can absorb more heat during the following day.

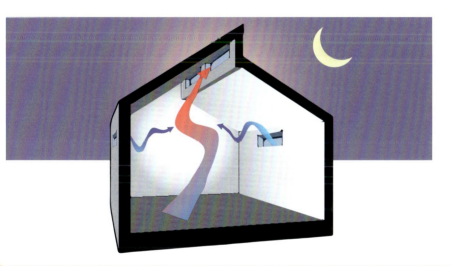

Fig. 42: Example of roof venting and stack ventilation examples

As process of heat absorption by thermal mass is slow, consequently the cooling down is also slow. Therefore, at night when outside temperature is cooler, night cooling is an effective way in removing absorbed heat from the thermal mass. In the same way, increasing night time ventilation can be considered as proper means in removing heat gain stored in structure of building during daytime.

Despite ventilation techniques, during hot months, it is important to use adequate shading and reduce daytime ventilation rates. Then it is possible to use night ventilation to remove absorbed heat in thermal mass (see Fig. 41–42).

There are some other innovative solutions to enhance night cooling such as:
- Using thermal mass of the bypassing air through the house structure (as an example bypassing air through hollow core slabs).
- Using a combination of roof venting and stack effect ventilation.

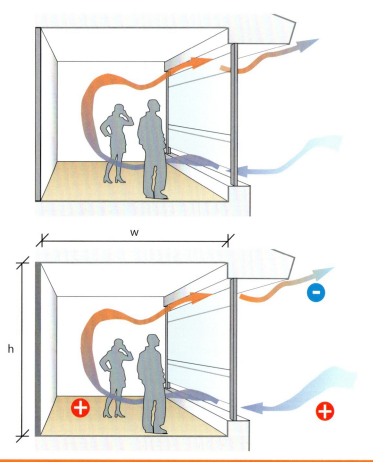

Fig. 43: Example of single-sided ventilation
Fig. 44: Wind effect (pressure driven) ventilation

However night cooling is a very effective way to use building envelope to remove absorbed heat during the day; the heat that is trapped inside the building and can reduce the affectivity of thermal mass in case of being not removed.

It should be mentioned that an appropriate window design has a strong influence on effectiveness of night cooling strategies (Özsen, Emma,. Lee, Tony,. 2010).

6.2 Types of Ventilation
Natural ventilation can be sorted out according to the numbers of openings, location of openings and times of ventilation. There are some commons types.

Single-sided ventilation
Single-side ventilation is referred to the type which openings are only in one side of space. This type is effective up to a certain depth of space (see Fig. 43–44). The common rules to calculate the depth of the space and size of the openings for effective ventilation are:
- Depth of room should not be bigger than 2.5 times the height (floor-to ceiling height).
- The open-able area should be at least 1/20th of ventilated floor area.

Cross-ventilation
Cross-ventilation type is referred to the type which open-able windows are on both sides of space (especially on opposite sides). It is functions due to the pressure difference between two sides of the building, namely where is facing the wind (windward side) and where is away from the wind (leeward side). The phenomenon which causes air movements through the building based on the positive pressure on the windward and negative pressure (vacuum) on the leeward side (see Fig. 45–46).

The movement of air through the building can be disruptive and causes draft problems. To avoid this effect, the open-able area of windows on the windward side should be less than open-able area of windows on the leeward side (see Fig. 47).

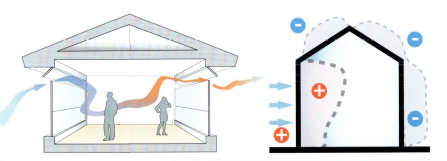

Fig. 45: Examples of cross-ventilation
Fig. 46: Pressure on windward and leeward sides

The common rules to calculate the depth of spaces and size of the openings for effective cross ventilation are:
- Depth of room should not be bigger than 5 times the height (floor to ceiling height).
- The open-able area on the windward side should be less than leeward side.

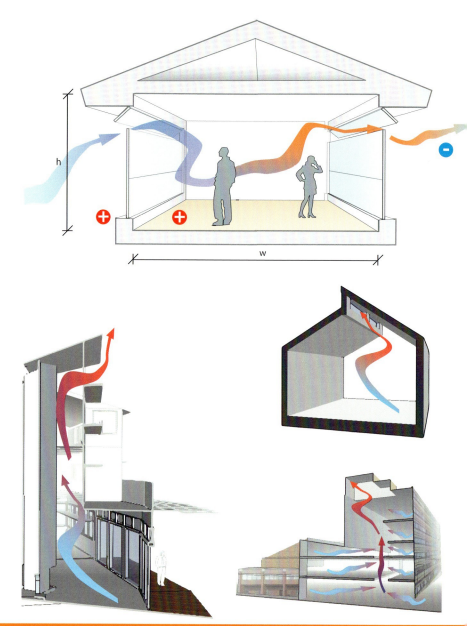

Fig. 47: For effective cross ventilation; W (maximum) approximately. 5 h
Fig. 48: Principle of stack ventilation and examples of stack ventilation by using solar chimney and through an atrium

Stack-effect ventilation
The stack-effect ventilation is referred to the type which uses the natural tendency of hot air to rise, to allow ventilation through high-level openings. This is more or less the same as smoke ventilation. It allows cooler fresh air to enter the building through lower openings.

This system can be optimized and improved through using some additional measures such as using: solar chimney, an atrium or double façade (see Fig. 48).

The idea behind the solar chimney is to create a column of air at a higher temperature which enhances the natural stack ventilation through the building. This is the same principle which supports using double façade the same as solar chimney (Özsen, Emma,. Lee, Tony,. 2010).

6.3 Design Consideration

There are various items affecting ventilation of a building. Therefore, appropriate ventilation design requires consideration of these items.

Building form

There is a considerable similarity between suitable shape for day-lighting and natural ventilation.

The following relationships among height, length and width of the space should be considered:

- In a building with possibility of cross ventilation, a natural ventilation strategy will be effective, when the distance between two openings is maximum 15 meters over an open-plan layout. However a long narrow floor plate functions better and is a more preferred form. It means the width (w) should be five times the room height (h).
- In a space with possibility of one-side ventilation, a natural ventilation strategy will be effective when the distance is maximum 7.5 m. However for ventilating a small room, one-side ventilation is an optimal strategy. It means the width (w) should be 2.5 times the room height (h) (see Fig. 49).

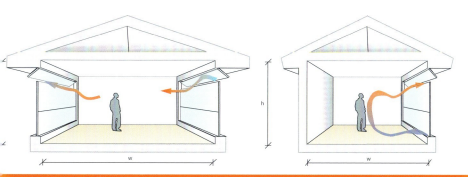

Fig. 49: Ventilation guidelines for room dimension

Windows and vents

The most common and the easiest way to make air exchange and let fresh air come in is opening the windows. This method suits most to small buildings where owner has control over the space. During windy or rainy days, when it is not possible to open the windows, ventilation could be provided through using adjustable louvers and small, thin (trickle) vents. However the choice should not be limited to only one option.

Atriums

Atriums are very old methods of providing ventilation, especially when it is not possible to provide natural ventilation from the perimeters, due to cultural, topographical or form obligations (see Fig. 50).

The height of atrium allows a temperature gradient and consequently creates air movements through stack effect. As warm air is rising to a higher level, outdoor air will flow into the buildings at the building perimeters.

There are certain sizes necessary for having effective atrium. Normally the area of atriums should not be less than 2 percent of the area that it is used to service. In case of a space limitation, a fairly small light-well can be used instead of a huge atrium.

Double-skin façade

In double skin façades, supply air enters the space (via the floor) and is warmed by internal gains.

Stack pressures within the two skins draw extract air at a higher level into the double-skin façade which is vented at the top of the building. Airflow in the façade can be significant, and blinds need to be restrained

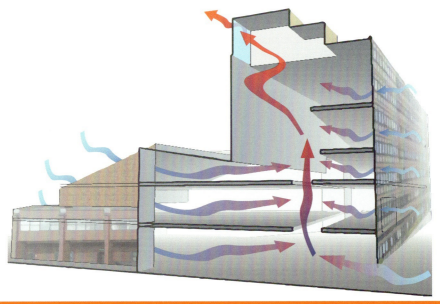

Fig. 50: A typical natural ventilation strategy with an internal atrium

to reduce rattling. Air is vented from the interior spaces into the façade through automated vents in the inner skin (see Fig. 51).

Ventilation and solar chimneys

The same as a light-well, a ventilation chimney will extend above roofline of a building to vent hot air through the stack effect or wind pressure (or both). The internal areas will be vented into the chimney.

To increase the temperature gradient within the chimney, solar chimney should be integrated with highly glazed areas. Therefore, glazed staircase can be used for this purpose.

Wind vanes
Among important considerations regarding ventilation are wind source at the site, the effect of building form on wind source and the devices to control and generate wind. Building form can facilitate the conduction of air into the space for absorption. Whereas such a strategy costs no additional expense for building, wind control devices (such as sails and wind vanes which should be extended into the airflow) and wind generators (such as

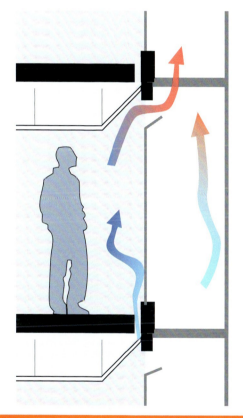

Fig. 51: typical natural ventilation strategies within a double-skin façade

turbines) will add to construction costs. Generally the followings should be considered:
- Even though there is a common trend to place turbines on the roof of the buildings, wind-flow over the top of a building is often turbulent and in low quality.
- Wind-flow around the corners of buildings is more reliable.

•• Wind-flow in the channeled flow between two neighboring buildings is more strong and reliable.

Evaporative cooling
In traditional architecture, in arid and semi-arid areas, very often there is a body of water in frame of pool which is placed in longest direction of inner courtyard. In fact, traditional architects were using evaporative cooling systems to create a more comfortable atmosphere in buildings. Therefore, incorporating a reasonable body of water into the site can effectively increase the cooling potentials of natural ventilation. The evaporation which occurs at the surface of water extracts heat from the air and, as the temperature of the air falls down; its relative humidity rises up. For effective evaporative cooling the followings should be considered:
•• The body of water would be more effective when it is placed at or near the outdoor air source.
•• To optimize evaporative cooling and movement of air and water, it is important to provide an extensive water-to-air contact, such as a pool which is stretched along the yard, the same like traditional houses.

Night purge
The night purge topic is associated with thermal mass, insulation and ventilation and should be considered in all those three topics. Regarding natural ventilation, the following points should be considered:
•• For effective night purge, the natural ventilation system should be performed during cooler night time temperatures.
•• Vents of used natural ventilation should be secured and closed in case of a bad weather (Ministry for Environment of New Zealand, 2008).

7 Airtightness

Air leakage or uncontrolled air exchange with external environment is among the main causes of heat loss within buildings. Air and consequently heated air can leave the building through a variety of paths. These paths can include porous building materials (such as block work), unsealed surface penetrations and ventilation ducts. However, it should be noticed that there is a difference between air leakage and ventilation. It should be mentioned that nearly half of all heat loss from an average constructed building is a result of uncontrolled air leakage through the gaps in the structure of the building. This phenomenon is absolutely different from controlled ventilation resulting from intentionally designed vents such as windows and fans (Morgan, Chris,. 2006).

7.1 General Principles

It is important, at this stage to; consider the differences between air infiltration and airtightness. These differences are best highlighted by looking at the factors on which figures airtightness and air infiltration are dependent. Air infiltration is not constant because it depends on a variety of factors including: wind direction, building orientation, ventilation strategy (e.g. mechanical or passive), internal to external temperatures and occupant behaviors. Many of the above factors are constantly changing, so air infiltration can (at best) only be estimated (Morgan, Chris,. 2006).

7.1.1 Myriad Way of Air Infiltration

There are many myriad ways in which air can infiltrate a building fabric.
1. Gaps between floor joists and inner leaf of external walls can connect with gaps throughout the building.
2. Gaps and poorly sealed membranes around, but especially beneath windows and window sills, leak direct to the outside or into the cavity.
3. Leakage through window openings due to ineffective or missing draught proofing, through hollow (plastic or metal) frames themselves.
4. Leakage through doors, especially the meeting stiles of double doors.
5. Gaps beneath and around doors.
6. Cracks around skirting boards linked to gaps around the edges of suspended floors.
7. Leakage through suspended floors, typically bare timber floor boards.
8. Gaps around loft hatches.
9. Leakage from eaves into attics often via cavities and behind plasterboard, indirectly into rooms.
10. Gaps around roof lights, e.g. where the roof light frame is not sealed to the adjacent rafters.

11. Cracks where dissimilar structural elements such as columns meet floor slabs.
12. Leakage through porous masonry leafs, e.g. prepends not filled, often linked to gaps behind dry-lining. In timber frame building e.g. where a vapur check is torn or not sealed.
13. Gaps in the external wall at services entry.
14. Leakage around ceiling roses, recessed spotlights and pull-cord switches between a warm room and roof space or intermediate floor.
15. Gaps around boiler flues (in walls and roofs).

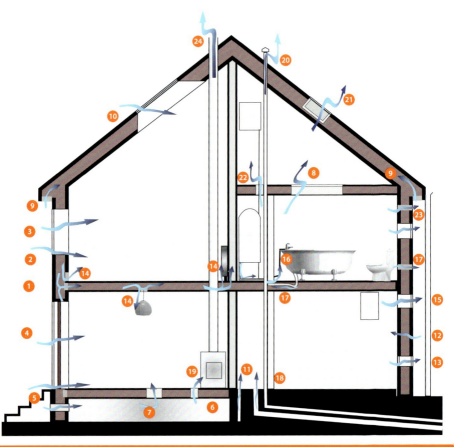

Fig. 52: Myriad way of air infiltration (Design & Detailing for Airtightness, Chris Morgan, SEDA 2006)

16. Small gaps where water/heating pipes enter rooms from floors, walls and boxed in spaces.
17. Gaps around waste pipe penetrations e.g. behind toilets, baths and kitchen sinks.
18. Service entry points, even in concrete slabs within a larger diameter pipe.

19. Airbrick/air entry to open-flued fires required by the regulations admits air at all times, not just when the fire is on use.
20. Large gaps where soil pipes/ventilation flues penetrate the roof.
21. Other roof penetrations e.g. overflow pipes.
22. Gaps between heated spaces and a cold loft where water pipes and cable cables pass between, often in airing cupboards.
23. Poorly sealed wall mounted extract fans, also ducted extract from cooker hoods; tumble driers etc. allow air directly into and out of the room, but also into the cavity.
24. Chimneys and flues, if not sealed properly will allow leakage at all times.

7.1.2 Standards for Air Leakage

Air leakage is quantified as air permeability (q50 value). This shows the rate of leakage expressed in cubic meters per hour per meter of envelope area ($m^3/(hr.m^2)$) in or out of the building. It is normally measured at a reference pressure difference of 50 Pascal (Pa) by a fan pressurization test (Morgan, Chris,. 2006).

7.2 Advantages of Airtight Building

There are several advantages associated with considering airtightness in a building.

Saving energy
Through reducing heat loss of building it is possible to consume less energy and even using smaller size of heating system which still meets the demanded temperature.

CO_2 emissions
As logical consequence of reducing energy loss of a building, an airtight building will ensure lower CO_2 emissions.

Improving internal level of comfort
Draughts and localized cold spots can cause discomfort, especially during cooler periods.

Improving sound insulation
Joints between elements and unwanted gaps in the building fabric are sealed as a part of air-tightness requirements. This reduces sound transmission, both from outside to inside of the building and also across the adjacent spaces.

Improving lifespan of building
An air tight building will reduce the likelihood of interstitial condensations and improve building fabric lifespan.

7.3 Design Consideration

For a well-constructed, well-insulated house, air leakage accounts for around 20–25% of the space heating energy use, so any reduction in heat loss from air leakage will have a significant benefit. Wind causes heat loss both through air leakage and by increasing the conduction heat loss, particularly through windows. There are therefore two primary ways of dealing with these heat losses:

- Making sure that building is well sealed, both in its construction joints and by weather stripping windows and doors.
- Using external wind breaks to reduce the impact of the wind on the building (these have the added advantage of making outdoor areas usable more often).

These should be used in combination. Weather-stripping cannot deal with increased heat loss by conduction through the glass itself, because the wind strips away the heat from the outer surface. Wind breaks can reduce this heat loss, but on their own, only partially solve air leak problems that weather-stripping addresses.

The main ways to deal with air leakage are:

- Using sheet materials or materials mortared together like brick or concrete walls which have fewer inherent leakage properties.
- Taking extra care during construction to seal all corner joints against air leakage.
- Ensuring penetrations in cladding or lining for plumbing or electrical fittings are well sealed.
- Where design and construction still allow possible air leakage, air-tightness barriers could be used. However, it is critical that they are vapor permeable and design and construction ensures that construction moisture will be dissipated and condensation from warm indoor air will not be trapped.

For a well air tight building these stages should be followed:

Performance specification
The performance specification allows an appropriate target to be set for the project, along with a description of how the process is to be conducted.

Zones and barriers
The next stage is to identify zones which require greater or lesser air-tightness levels (for example heated zones need to be kept separate from unheated zones such as roof voids, delivery bays etc.).

Designing air barrier
After defining zones and air barrier it is necessary to design air barriers. To be effective, the air barrier must:

- Be made of suitably air impermeable materials.

- Be continuous around the envelope or zone.
- Have sufficient strength to withstand any pressure created by wind, stack effect or air control systems.
- Be easily installable.
- Be durable.
- Be accessible for maintenance/replacement if necessary (Morgan, Chris,. 2006).

1. Heating could be provided through under floor heating systems or by direct sun radiation and solar heat inside the rooms.
2. It should be mentioned that used wood could be affected by moisture and insects.
3. As finishing, all standard systems can be used, systems such as: masonry veneers, weatherboards and plaster finishing systems.
4. As mentioned before, close to exterior surface of walls.
5. Polystyrene sheets are prefitted inside the blocks near exterior surface.
6. Here, the important issue is ensuring that moisture could be dissipated and it is possible to prevent trapping of condensation from warm indoor air.
7. They could have different colors such as: silver, gold, bronze and etc.
8. Normally the blockage of light is more than heat.
9. Thermal mass could be more effective when it receives direct sunlight and also when it has dark colors which can absorb more heat.
10. Absorbed and stored heat would be released back to the air, when the temperature of space drops down and to less than thermal mass temperature.
11. It should be mentioned that conductivity should not be very high, as an example, even though steel has a very high conductivity, but it absorbs and gives off energy so quickly that cannot create any delay effect that is the main reason for using a thermal mass.
12. When the walls are built with considerable amounts of thermal mass, the more reflective floor can be more effective. As such a floor will reflect the heat and will distribute it to the walls, which can be more easily cooled down at night (since they are exposed to cooler night-time temperatures).
13. In general, light which reaches a task indirectly (such as having bounced from a white wall) will provide a better lighting quality than light which arrives directly from a natural or artificial source.
14. Naturally human eye is attracted to an area where there is contrast in brightness. The attraction to the brighter area could be useful in guiding people towards main areas opposite the uniform and boring corridors.
15. The option for mechanical system can vary as from a simple fan to a fairly complex and expensive system.

VI
Appendix

List of References

A background to running a sustainable housing project, http://www.sustainableconstruction.co.uk.

Ahmadi-Nedoshan, Afshin,. Abedi, Afshin,. Talebi, Mansour:
Approach to energy efficiency for cooling in residential buildings, 6th National Energy Congress, Iran, 2007.

Al-Asir, hala shaker,. Awadallah, Tala,. Blomsterberger, Ake,. Hakansson, Hakan,. Hellström, Bengt,. Kvist, Hasse:
Climate Conscious Architecture and urban design in Jordan, Media-Tryck. Lund, 2009.

Al. Homoud, Mohammad S.:
Performance characteristics and practical applications of common building thermal insulation materials, ELSEVIRE, 2004.

Andresen, Inger:
A Multi-criteria Decision Making Method for Solar Building Design, Phd Thesis, Norwegian University of Science and Technology faculty of architecture Planning and Fine Arts Department of Building Technology, 2000.

bere:architects:
Airtightness Report, UK, 2012.

Bentil, Daniel:
Alternative Resdential Construction Systems, Second edition, College of Design construction and planning, University of Florida, 2001.

Brown, Marilyn A.,. Southworth, Frank,. Stovall, Therese K:
Solutions Towards a Climate-Friendly Built Environment, Oak Ridge National Laboratory, USA, 2005.

Buckley, Mike,. Halsall, Robert,. Vollering, Brennan,. Webber, Doug:
Considering sustainability in the selection of structural systems, Halsall Associates Limited, Canada.

Building System Comparison:
www.duralitegreen.com.

BCA, Building & Construction Authority:
Design Guide on Use of Alternative Structural Steel, 2012.

BCA, Building & Construction Authority:
Quality Features in Structural Elements.

BCA, Building & Construction Authority:
Quality Homes.

CABE & Richards Partington Architects:
Applying housing standards: London case studies, 2010.

CAM, Client Assistance Memo:
Sustainable Building and reuse of Building Materials, Department of Planning and development of Seattle, 2001.

Chester, Matthew:
A Road Map to energy Efficient Building Codes: Which Path Do We Take?, University of Virginia, 2009.

Chudley, Roy:
Advanced Construction Technology, Vol. I, II, III, IV, Longman Group Limited, 3rd edition, 1999

CIRS (UBC Center for Interactive Research on Sustainability):
Building materials, The University of British Columbia, 2011.

Climate and Comfort—Passive Design Strategies for Lebanon, UNDP, 2005.

Construction Systems Comparison:
www.aeconline.ae.

Crosbi, Tracy,. Dawood, Nashwan,. Dean, John:
Energy Profiling in the Life-cycle assessment of Buildings, University of Teesside, UK, 2010

Crosbi, Tracy,. dawood, Nashwan,. Dean, John,.:
A Framework and Decision Support System to Increase Building life Cycle energy Performance, University of Teesside, UK, www.itcon.org, 2010.

Dekay, Mark:
Teachning with Sun, Wind, & Light, University of Tennessee, 2001.

Dincel Construction Systems Pty Ltd.:
Cost Saving Summary and Risk Assessment.

Donn, Michael,. Grant, Thomas:
Designing Comfortable Homes, 2nd Edition, Cemnet & Concrete association of New Zealand, 2010.

eco buildings:
EU FP6 Eco Buildings Symposium paper, Fraunhofer Institut für Bauphysik, www.ecobuildings.info 2005.

eco buildings:
2nd EU FP6 Eco Buildings Symposium papers, Stuttgart, www.ecobuildings.info, 2008.

eCubed Building Workshop Ltd:
Passive Solar Design Guidelines, Ministry for Environment of New Zealand, 2008.

eCubed Building Workshop Ltd.:
Integrated Whole Building Design Guidelines, Ministry for Environment of New Zealand, 2008.

Eliasson, Ingegärd:
The Use of climate Knowledge in Urban planning, ELSEVIER, 2000.

Energy Star:
Series of online products "Advanced LightingPackage, Appliance, Cooling, Duct System, Heating, Insulation, Lighting, Mechanical Ventilation, Water Heaters, Windows, Independent Inspection and Testing, a U.S. Environmental Protection Agency Program, http://www.energystar.gov/.

Erhorn-Kluttig, Heike,. Erhorn, Hans:
Innovative Insulation, Fraunhofer Institut für BauPhysik, EU 6th framework programme Eco-building, Guidelines, www.ecobuildings.info, 2007.

Erhorn, Hans,. Ole Hansen, Jens,. Kaan, Henk,. Barker, Mike:
What are Eco- buildings and are they needed in the Seventh Framework Programm (FP7)?, BRITA in PUBs, 2007.

Erell, Evyatar,. Pearlmutter, David,. Williamson, Terry:
City Weathers; Meteorology and Urban Design, Manchester Architect Research Center (MARC), UK, 2010.

Fanger, P. Ole:
What is IAQ? Indoor Air, 2006; 16.

Fullbrook, David:
Sustainable Government Buildings, eCubed Building Workshop Ltd, New Zealand, 2007.

Ghazizadeh, S. Neda., Monam, A. & Mahmoodi, A. S.:
The Impact of the Architectural Design on the Thermal Comfort of the Outdoor Spaces in Residential Complexes. Honar-ha-ye-Ziba, 42, 59–70, 2010.

Haglund, Bruce,. Rathmann, Kurt:
Thermal mass in Passive Solar and Energy-Conserving Buildings, 1996.

Hasting, S.R.:
Passive Solar Commerical and Institutional Buildings: A Sourcebook of Examples and Design Insights, International Energy Agency, France. John Wiley and Sons, 1994.

High Performance House:
Best Practices Guide, NYSERDA, https://www.nyserda.ny.gov.

High Performance manufactured Housing:
Environmental and energy Study Institute, EESI, 2011.

Hugan, John C.:
Sustainable Design Guide, Los Almos National Laboratory Sustainable Design Guide, USA, 2012.

Indriksone, Daina,. Bremere, Ingrida,. Aleksejeva, Irina,. Grätz, Matthias,. Oisalu, Sandra,. Svirskaite, Justina:
Using ecological construction materials in the Baltic States, Baltic Environment Forum (BEF), 2011.

Kalkan, Erol,. Yüksel, S. Bahadir:
Pros and Cons of Multistory RC Tunnel-Form (Box-Type) Buildings, Published online in Wiley Interscience, www.interscience.wiley.com, 2007.

Kang, Grace S.,. Kren, Alan:
Structural Engineering Strategies Towards Sustainable Design, SEAONC, 2007.

Knauf Insulation Ltd.:
Key Insulation Design Considerations.

Land Use Consultants, levett-Therivel:
Sustainable Construction in Cambridgeshire A Good Practice Guide, 2006.

Lawrence Berkeley National Laboratory:
Selecting Windows for Energy Efficiency, U.S. Department of Energy.

Lightweight Structure Association:
Lightweight Structures for efficient and Sustainable Building Solution courses.

Los Alamos National Laboratory:
Sustainable Design, www.lanl.gov.

Machado, Maria V.,. La Roche, Pablo M.:
Materials and appropriate design strategies for building in hot climates.

Madsen, Travis,. Wohlschlegel, Kari,. Kohler, Dan:
Wisconsin's Clean Energy Future, Wisconsin Environment Reaserch & Policy Center, 2009.

Markus, T., Morris, E.:
Buildings, Climate and Energy, London, Pitman 1980.

Melki, Habib:
Windows ae Environmental Modifiers in Lebaneses Vernacular Architecture, PLEA2006—The 23rd Conference on Passive and Low Energy Architecture, Switzerland, 2006.

Ministry for the Environment of New Zealand:
Sustainable Building case Study: Conservation House Whare Kaupapa Atawhai, New Zealand, 2007.

Monam, Alireza:
The Dependence of Outdoor Thermal Comfort on Urban Layout, Young Cities Research Brief, Berlin, 2013.

Monam, Alireza:
Comfortability in Urban Open Spaces; Evaluation of Outdoor Thermal Comfort in Urban Parks. PhD, Iran university of science and technology, 2011.

Monam, A. & Ghazizadeh, S. N.:
Effects of Urban Layouts and Landscape Parameters on Outdoor Thermal Comfort. The 32nd International Geographical Congress. Cologne, Germany, 2012.

Morgan, Chris:
Design and Detailing for Airtightness, SEDA design Guides for Scotland: No.2; 2006.

Nilforoushan, Mohammadreza,. Raid, Hena,. Sadeghi Naeini, Hassan:
Application of innovative sustainable methods for daylighting, 2th improving energy consumption patterns, Iran, 2010.

O'Connor, Jennifer,. Lee, Eleanor,. Rubinstein, Francis,. Selkowitz, Stephen:
Tips for Daylighting with Windows, 1998.

Okeil, Ahmad:
A holistic approach to energy efficient building form, ELSEVIER, 2010.

Özsen, Emma,. Lee, Tony:
Passive Solar Design Guidelines, 1st edition, 2010, Ministry of energy and Public Utilities of Mauritius & Danish Energy management A/S.

Ratti, Carlo,. Dana, Raydan,. Steemers, Koen:
Building Form and Environmental performance: Archetypes Analysis and an Arid Climate, ELSEVIER, 2003.

Rinaldi, Nicola:
Thermal Mass, Night Cooling and Hollow Core Ventilation System as Energy Saving strategies in Building, Ms Thesis, KTH-Sweden, 2009

Rural Structure in the Tropics
Designs and Development, 2011, www.fao.org.

Saberi, Ommid,. Saneei, Parisa,. Javanbakht, Amir:
Thermal Comfort in Architecture, NCEUB, www.nceub.commoncense.info.

Salazar Rellihan, Sara:
Design with Climate: A Retreat for Vieques Puerto Rico, Ms Thesis, University of Maryland, 2003.

Scottsdale Green Building Program:
Passive Design Strategies, 2005.

Shahmohammadi, Fatemeh,. Azimi, Aziz,. kazemzadeh- Hanani, Siamak:
Simulation and improvement Building of heating energy consumption, 5th Improvement of Fuel Consumption in Building Congress, Iran, 2006.

St. Clair, Peter:
Guidelines for climate responsive Design in Cold Climates with Particular References to Beijing, China.

St. Clair, Peter:
Low-Energy Design in the United Arab Emirates, DES 30, 2009.

Stroh, Robert:
Alternative Residential Construction Systems, 2nd Edition, University of Florida, 2001.

The Concrete Center:
High Performance Buildings—Using Tunnel Form Concrete Construction, UK, 2004.

The Wisconsin Energy Star Homes Program:
Standards and Guidelines for New Home Construction, www.focusonenergy.com

The Interagency Sustainability Working Group (ISWG):
High performance and Sustainable Buildings Guidance, www.wbdg.org, USA, 2008.

Tilghman, M. Tench:
Constructing a Successful Residential Green Rating Guideline, Master degree Thesis, University of Florida, 2006.

UKTFA:
The e-Center, Timber Frame Construction.

UNEP:
Buildings and Climate Change, Status, Challenges and Opportunities, 2007.

Westbury, Philippa:
A Sense of place, CABE, 2007.

List of Figures

Fig. 1:	Solar radiation in different orientations	30
Fig. 2:	Solar altitude of Tehran	31
Fig. 3:	Maximizing glazing on south orientation and using benefits of a sloped site for shading façades exposed to direct sun	32
Fig. 4:	Example use of landscape to control flow of wind into a house	32
Fig. 5:	Proper building orientation on north-south and building elongation on east-west axis	33
Fig. 6:	Effectiveness of shading by overhangs	34
Fig. 7:	Effectiveness of using plants for shading	35
Fig. 8:	Function of sunspaces in winter and summer	38
Fig. 9:	Values of embodied energy for most common construction materials [MJ/kg]	72
Fig. 9:	Values of embodied energy for most common construction materials [MJ/kg]	84
Fig. 11:	Guidance for windows orientation	105
Fig. 12:	Example of triple glazing	108
Fig. 13:	Example of efficient window	111
Fig. 14:	Guidance for windows size in different direction	113
Fig. 15:	How thermal mass can moderate temperature fluctuations (Design Comfortable Home)	116
Fig. 16:	A trombe wall	118
Fig. 17:	the internal structure of transparent insulation	119
Fig. 18:	A thermal labyrinth and a rockbin	120
Fig. 19:	Thermal mass application	121
Fig. 20:	Building footprints for best daylight access	126

Fig. 21:	Daylighting guidelines for room dimensions	127
Fig. 22:	The use of a sloped ceiling to improve daylight penetration into a room	128
Fig. 23:	The effect of shading to limit sunlight penetration into a room	129
Fig. 24:	Effectiveness and function of overhang in summer and winter	130
Fig. 25:	Example of heat transmission through windows	131
Fig. 26:	Example of simple shading	132
Fig. 27:	Example of cost effective shading strategies for east or west sides	133
Fig. 28:	Allowing sun penetration in winter	134
Fig. 29:	Examples of movable shading (adjustable awning and roller shutter blinds)	135
Fig. 30:	Examples of using trees as shading devices	136
Fig. 31:	Examples of use of clerestories for daylight	138
Fig. 32:	Examples of use of light shelf as a reflector	139
Fig. 33:	Overhangs (left) and sidefins (right)	140
Fig. 34:	Horizontal and vertical louvres	141
Fig. 35:	A green-screen with the two meshes hung on the solid façade	142
Fig. 36:	Shading strategies within a double skin façade, with blinds hung between the two glazing skins.	143
Fig. 37:	Applicable measures	144
Fig. 38:	Different location of opening for natural ventilation	145
Fig. 39:	Matching opening type to roof pitch	146
Fig. 40:	Wind effect (pressure driven) ventilation (left), stack effect (temperature driven) ventilation (right)	147
Fig. 41:	Stack ventilation examples	148
Fig. 42:	Example of roof venting and stack ventilation examples	149
Fig. 43:	Example of single-sided ventilation	150
Fig. 44:	Wind effect (pressure driven) ventilation	150
Fig. 45:	Examples of cross-ventilation	151
Fig. 46:	Pressure on windward and leeward sides	151

Fig. 47: For effective cross ventilation; W (maximum) approximately 152

Fig. 48: Principle of stack ventilation and examples of stack ventilation by using solar chimney and through an atrium. 152

Fig. 49: Ventilation guidelines for room dimension. 153

Fig. 50: A typical natural ventilation strategy with an internal atrium 154

Fig. 51: typical natural ventilation strategies within a double-skin façade. 155

Fig. 52: Myriad way of air infiltration (Design & detailing for Airtightness, Chris Morgan, SEDA 2006) 158

List of Tables

Tab. 1:	Energy consumption in transportation of materials	74
Tab. 2:	Influence of frames, glazing panes and spacers on U-Factor (U.S. Department of Energy)	106
Tab. 3:	Comparison of glass types according visible transmittance, U-factor and solar heat gain coefficient (Passive Solar Design Guidelines)	112

Abbreviations

AAC	Autoclaved Aerated Concrete
BHRC	Building and Housing Research Center
BMBF	German Federal Ministry of Education and Research
CMMU	Community Management and Monitoring Unit
CW	Constructed Wetlands
EPS	Expanded Polystyrene
ETICS	External thermal Insulation Composite System
FSC	Forest Stewardship Council
HIC	Housing Investment Company
MDF	Medium Density Fibreboard
NTDC	The New Towns Development Corporation of Iran
OSB	Oriented Strand Board
pph.	person per hectare
PUR	Polyurethane
PVC	Polyvinychlorid
RC	Reinforced Concrete
SA:V	surface-area-to-volume
SHGC	Solar Heat Gain Coefficient
UFFI	Urea-formaldehye Foam Insulation
UV	Ultraviolet
UNDP	United Nation Development Programme
XPS	Extruded Polystyrene

Young Cities Project Consortium

Technische Universität Berlin
Berlin, Germany

Road, Housing & Urban Development Research Center of Iran
(*former Building and Housing Research Center, BHRC*)
Tehran, Islamic Republic of Iran

New Towns Development Corporation
Tehran, Islamic Republic of Iran

Iranian Ministry of Roads & Urban Development (MRUD)
(*former Ministry of Housing and Urban Development, MHUD*)
Tehran, Islamic Republic of Iran

Atmospheric Science and Meteorological Research Center
Tehran, Islamic Republic of Iran

Berlin University of the Arts
Berlin, Germany

young cities
Developing Urban Energy Efficiency
Tehrān-Karaj

FIRST Fraunhofer
Institute for Computer Architecture
and Software Technology
Berlin, Germany

Freie Universität Berlin
Berlin, Germany

inter3 Institute for Resource
Management GmbH
Berlin, Germany

nexus Institute for Cooperation
Management & Interdisciplinary
Research GmbH
Berlin, Germany

p2m berlin GmbH
Berlin, Germany

Vocational Advancement Service of the
Berlin-Brandenburg Construction Industry
Association
Potsdam, Germany

About the Authors

Prof. Dr.-Ing. Klaus Rückert
Prof. Dr.-Ing. Klaus Rückert is Head of the chair of Design and Structures and managing Vice Director of the Department of Architecture at the Technische Universität Berlin in Germany.

He graduated in Civil and Structural Engineering at the University of Stuttgart, Germany and subsequently in Civil Engineering at University of California, Berkeley, USA. He is professionally engaged in international and transnational research and implementation projects of sustainable building design in Europe, Africa, Latin America and Asia. Parallel with his task as Team 3 leader in Young Cities project, he developed and managed the Longlife and the pilot cluster initiative "Energy efficiency and renewable energy sources" projects, both in Baltic sea Region Program 2007–13.

Prof. Dr. -Ing. Klaus Rückert is CEO and shareholder of the engineering company PRB Rückert Planers and Consultants, Heilbronn and Berlin, Germany. Prof. Dr.-Ing. Klaus Rückert is an appointed proof engineer for stability of the State and City of Berlin in the field of steel and solid constructions. In his professional carrier, he has been involved in the realization of a great number and big variety of construction projects such as bridges, industrial and health care buildings and listed historical buildings.

He is an expert in energy efficient design and earthquake resistant engineering. Since 2011 he is President of the Longlife Institute e.V., an association getting involved for sustainable, energy efficient and resource saving buildings with respect to certification and life cycle analysis.

He is also a member of various national and international organizations.

Effatolsadat Shahriari

Effatolsadat Shahriari is Young Cities Research associate at the chair of Design and Structures, chair of Prof. Dr. -Ing. Klaus Rückert, at the Department of Architecture at the Technische Universität Berlin in Germany.

She obtained her Master's degree in Architecture and Urbanism from the Iran University of Science & Technology in Tehran. She got her NDS diploma from ETH Zürich in Urbanism with "Open Spaces in Contemporary Cities" as the main topic. She has worked for several years as an assistant in the University of Science & Technology, school of architecture and urbanism and as a research assistant in the center of architecture & urban studies of University of Science & Technology in Tehran.

She is professionally dedicated to the sustainable research projects, especially residential research projects from both architectural and urban aspect.

Since 2010, Effat Shahriari has joined Young Cities research team while at the same time she was active as a research associate in Longlife research project (Sustainable, energy efficient and resource saving residential buildings around Baltic Sea sponsored by EU) and Longlife design class.

She has taken part in different seminars and workshops as an expert for energy efficient building, material and structure as well as difficulties related to the development of new cities in Iran and MENA region.